THE COMPLETE BOOK OF
CANDLES
AND CANDLEMAKING

THE COMPLETE BOOK OF
CANDLES
AND CANDLEMAKING

150 practical projects and fabulous decorative displays

GLORIA NICOL

LORENZ BOOKS

This edition is published by Lorenz Books

Lorenz Books is an imprint of Anness Publishing Ltd
Hermes House, 88–89 Blackfriars Road, London SE1 8HA
tel. 020 7401 2077; fax 020 7633 9499
www.lorenzbooks.com; info@anness.com

© Anness Publishing Ltd 1999, 2004

UK agent: The Manning Partnership Ltd, 6 The Old Dairy, Melcombe Road, Bath BA2 3LR; tel. 01225 478444; fax 01225 478440; sales@manning-partnership.co.uk

UK distributor: Grantham Book Services Ltd, Isaac Newton Way, Alma Park Industrial Estate, Grantham, Lincs NG31 9SD;
tel. 01476 541080; fax 01476 541061; orders@gbs.tbs-ltd.co.uk

North American agent/distributor: National Book Network, 4501 Forbes Boulevard, Suite 200, Lanham, MD 20706;
tel. 301 459 3366; fax 301 429 5746; www.nbnbooks.com

Australian agent/distributor: Pan Macmillan Australia, Level 18, St Martins Tower, 31 Market St, Sydney, NSW 2000;
tel. 1300 135 113; fax 1300 135 103; customer.service@macmillan.com.au

New Zealand agent/distributor: David Bateman Ltd, 30 Tarndale Grove, Off Bush Road, Albany, Auckland;
tel. (09) 415 7664; fax (09) 415 8892

A CIP catalogue record for this book is available from the British Library.

Publisher: Joanna Lorenz
Project Editor: Zoe Antoniou
Editor: Judy Cox
Designer: Julie Francis
Editorial Reader: Joy Wotton
Production Controller: Wendy Lawson
Special Photography: Debbie Patterson

Previously published as *The Complete Book of Candles*

Picture credits: Page 1 shows a selection of beeswax candles and pots of honey; page 2 shows beeswax candles with a basket of lavender; page 3 shows golden brown candles with seasonal flowers; page 4 shows an embossed candle in a seaside setting; and page 5 shows (clockwise from top) candles in painted gold bowls, candles decorated with pressed flowers, yellow floating candle, mosaic candleholder, painted candleholder, red floating rose candles and green coloured candle.

1 3 5 7 9 10 8 6 4 2

IMPORTANT NOTE
Please take care at all times to ensure that candles are firmly secured and that lighted candles are never
left unattended. Please also take care when making candles as hot wax can be dangerous.

Contents

Introduction

ABOVE Brightly coloured and twisted candles make a lavish display next to fresh flowers that are complementary in hue.

There is currently a huge revival of interest in candles, with specialist shops supplying every imaginable shape and colour and many different types of candleholder. This abundance of inspiration makes it very easy to decorate with candles throughout your home and also outdoors, changing the colours and displays to reflect the seasons.

Even when unlit, a simple design such as a candle pot will decorate a dull corner. In the evening, the candlelight will transform any room, instantly creating mood and atmosphere. Candles symbolize light, warmth and hospitality, and are thus invaluable for entertaining either a few friends with an informal meal or a roomful of guests at a large party. On festive occasions during the year, such as Christmas and Easter, candles are a traditional and indispensable part of the decorations, and the flickering candlelight conveys a sense of magic and wonder that cannot be replaced. It is simple to create new displays for these familiar festivals by using different colours and adding interesting accessories. One of the beauties of working with candles is that you can start again with something new each time.

This book begins with an inspirational section containing many different ideas for using and displaying candles. These are arranged by theme so that you can quickly find a suggestion for each season of the year, or for a special event, colour scheme or mood, such as Pure Gold or Country Style. Making Candles describes how to make your own candles, giving you the freedom to combine exactly the dye colours and

ABOVE The combination of fire and water makes a dazzling display, and floating candles are particularly safe for a party.

designs you wish. It also includes some lovely ideas for decorating
ready-made candles to turn them into something special. Any of these
hand-made candles would make an ideal, personal gift that would
certainly be appreciated.

Creative Candleholders shows the range of holders you can make or
decorate, from a simple salt dough candlestick to a jewelled candelabra.
There are designs here for every mood and every event, from classic
simplicity to over-the-top extravaganza. Candles lend themselves to bold
and romantic theatrical gestures, which by the next morning have
disappeared in a puff of smoke.

It is always important to take precautions with candles, especially at
a party. Always be very careful when the candles are lit and never leave
them unattended. Remove the candles before they burn down to the
level of any decorative material, such as dried flowers, and replace them
with new ones. Enclosed candleholders, such as lanterns, are much
safer than a naked flame, and floating candles in a large bowl of water

ABOVE Once candles have been dipped in a
favourite colour, they can be personalized
with extravagant, carved designs, making the
most creative and attractive gifts.

ABOVE Imaginations can run wild when
making candles to create special effects, such
as marbled wax.

ABOVE Candles are easily decorated with ornate designs made from flower petals.

ABOVE Church (ivory pillar) candles burn longer than paraffin-based candles, making them ideal for decorative designs.

are another good choice at a party. Place candles out of reach so that they will not be in danger of being knocked over and check that they are stable, supporting them with other material in the display. Make sure the candles fit well in the candleholders without wobbling. If necessary, apply a little candle fix to the bottom of the candle to hold it firmly upright. This soft, sticky wax is available in small tins or as flat beads in a packet. If the candle is too large, you can shave off thin strips of wax from around the base with a knife.

Another practical consideration is how to store candles. Bundles of white candles tied with wide ribbon look very decorative on display on a shelf or in a basket, but be careful to keep coloured candles out of direct sunlight otherwise the lovely colours will fade unevenly. Ideally, store candles horizontally on a cupboard shelf or in a drawer, away from the light. Do not store them anywhere warm, since the wax will melt and the shape will become distorted. Dipped taper candles are traditionally hung up in pairs from a single length of wick on a peg or nail in the wall; they

LEFT Nightlights (tea-lights) in glass containers let out a particularly soft light that is sure to create a warm and romantic setting. Place them amongst flowers and vegetables in the garden or hang them in a selection of coloured jars from trees.

make a very attractive decoration but, again, remember to keep them out of the sunlight. It is always worth having a selection of candles in store. When unexpected guests arrive, you can simply add a collar of dried herbs or lavender made the previous summer, or pick a few fresh flowers or even vegetables from the garden.

Using candles outdoors on warm summer evenings is one of the most magical ways to display them. Scented candles, such as those made with citronella oil, will help keep away unwelcome insects. Sweet-scented candles will mingle with the heady perfume of honeysuckle, jasmine and roses. The other great place for scented candles is in the bathroom, where essential oils such as lavender or rosemary can make you feel truly pampered. As candles have become more popular, we have learnt how to use them, how to experiment with them and how to enjoy their full potential in many new and stimulating ways.

ABOVE Gilded candle displays are simply stunning and well worth making, and they need not be too expensive.

INSPIRATIONAL

candle displays

Choose different coloured candles and different styles of candleholder to celebrate the changing seasons of the year and to complement your home and lifestyle. Create lovely displays on special occasions such as dinner parties, weddings and anniversaries, and of course at Christmas.

Introduction

ABOVE Pure white candles and candleholders combine with white flowers to create a stunning wedding display.

Whether you are decorating a corner of your living room or planning a large outdoor party, there is sure to be a particular candle or candle display that will be right for the occasion. Once we looked to flowers to provide a splash of colour and create a focal point, but now we have discovered that candles can fulfil the same role.

For everyday decorating, place small candle pots in cheerful colours on a side table or telephone table. Use them to brighten up a dark

BELOW A plain candle puts a finishing touch to a country-style setting, together with lavender bags and a woven basket.

corner, changing the display as you would a vase of flowers to keep the idea fresh and interesting. You can use the same candleholder repeatedly, but with different candles and accessories to make it look completely different. Add a few herbs as they come into season, or quickly tie with a ribbon or raffia bow to dress it up for visitors. Collect a stock of useful accessories, looking to various sources such as the Shakers or folk art, for inspiration. When you have decorated the living room, aromatic herb candles are lovely in the kitchen and scented candles are blissfully self-indulgent in the bedroom and bathroom.

For special events, candles are associated with festive occasions, such as Christmas and birthdays, so they always create a feeling of

LEFT Special moulded candles in fish shapes or shells are particularly fun to make and use.

celebration and well-being. A candelabra or chandelier is the ultimate grand gesture, and you can vary the same base by decorating it with trailing ivy or gold leaves. Dark colours such as burgundy or deep blue create quite a different effect to elegant cream or pale gold. If you are feeling really inventive, you can make your own candelabra or chandelier out of builder's materials or adapt an old one found in a junkshop or in the attic. Alternatively, create an impressive display at a dinner party by piling up exotic fruits, gorgeous fresh flowers and large leaves in the centre of the table, placing the candles to focus attention on them. Designs of this kind have no base structure, and each display is original.

On still, warm summer evenings, outdoor entertaining is transformed by twinkling lights positioned around the garden or grouped together on a party table. Lanterns and enclosed lights are best here as they won't blow out if there is any wind. Outdoor candleholders can be extremely simple, and recycled glass jars and tins look quite bewitching in the candlelight. When you are working with candles, remember that glass and metal of all kinds will sparkle and shine once the candles are lit. Guests will be delighted with unusual containers and with novel or special decorations, such as the combination of fire and water with tiny floating candles.

ABOVE Floating candles bring fire and water together for an effect that is simply magical.

BELOW Such is the beauty of flickering candlelight that even the simplest of glass containers can be dazzling.

rainbow

■ ■ ■ ■

Candle wax can be easily dyed to every colour imaginable, and there
is now a huge range available. Use bold colours such as scarlet or
gold to make an impact, or choose natural colours to complement
flowers and foliage in a rustic display.

GLOWING
gold

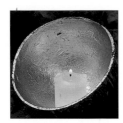

More than any other colour, gold reflects candlelight to create a shimmering glow that is truly magical. For a special occasion such as a wedding or anniversary, gold candles always look luxurious when combined in a stunning display, perhaps with white lilies or yellow mimosa. Alternatively, a gold candle simply displayed at home will bring this feeling of celebration and extravagance into your everyday lifestyle.

Gold candles can be used to create quite a range of different effects. You can mix gold candles with shades of white, cream and natural colours in a modern interior or, to achieve quite a contrasting atmosphere, use rich gold candles with deep reds and

ABOVE Decorate the corner of a Christmas mantelpiece with gold-sprayed fruit and leaves, then add a single gold candle for a simple, elegant effect. Gold and white make a beautiful colour scheme that is particularly suited to the festive season.

RIGHT The subtle touch of gold leaf gives these cream candles a luxurious richness. Delicate filigree patterns are quite easy to draw on to the candles, and they suit the medieval character of the gold colour.

LEFT For a weathered, rustic look, unevenly spray a collection of attractive-shaped objects, including a candlestick, with gold spray paint so that the original colour shows through in places. The candlelight will bathe them in a lovely warm glow.

BELOW Dark green and gold work especially well together, giving a touch of exotic splendour. Display a pair of these candles on a dark wooden dining table or on either end of a mantelpiece at Christmas or New Year.

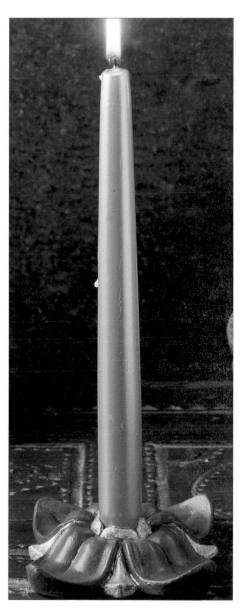

greens to create a more exotic style. Choose simple, Grecian-style candles or ornately decorated candles to create very different moods, depending on the occasion. Rich, spicy aromas such as cinnamon, frankincense and myrrh complement the gold colours perfectly, and will send ripples of colour and scent through your home.

At Christmas, gold candles symbolize the magic and enchantment of this special time of year. Surround them with pine cones and other woodland materials gilded with gold spray paint, or make an Advent candle to last throughout the build-up to Christmas. Arrange gold candles with gold accessories to build up a lavish assembly of objects for a dinner table or a mantelpiece display.

C O O L silver

Plain white candles combine beautifully with glass and silver, the light of the candles reflecting icily in their smooth, cool surfaces. Traditional silver candlesticks and candelabra are still a lovely, elegant way to display candles, but nowadays modern interiors are just as likely to use punched tin candleholders or recycled metal containers. The idea is to experiment with shiny surfaces that reflect the light and look good as a backdrop to your candles. Similarly, antique cut glass refracts the light to create a dazzling display, but less expensive glass often works just as well. Even a humble glass jam jar can look magical in the shimmering candlelight.

LEFT This decorative candle sconce is ingeniously made out of cake tins and biscuit moulds. The combination of a simple white candle, silvery metal and scalloped shapes is very pleasing.

BELOW Create an enchanting effect with delicate candle collars cut out of aluminium foil, scored with different designs and decorated with beads. These delightful collars will dress up glass candlesticks for a special evening display.

Lacy candleholders and scalloped shapes combine with silver to create a rather Elizabethan look, which is otherwise best kept very restrained as far as colour is concerned. White candles, silver and glass always look right, whatever the surroundings and on any occasion. For a special display, simply pile up faceted glass, shiny metallic materials and mirrors around a group of candles so that the rays of light really twinkle back and forth. Add some delicate silver-sprayed seed heads if you want to introduce a natural element. This kind of display looks quite magical at Christmas decorated with silver-frosted pine cones and a few silver tree decorations. Experiment with intricate silver-coloured decorations to emphasize the delicate aspect of candlelight.

LEFT The silvery glow from a homemade tin lantern will welcome guests to your home or provide light for a garden party. The lantern is open on one side, but the flame is well protected behind and at the sides, so that it can safely be left outdoors.

CREAMY white

Some of the loveliest candles are those in subtle complementary shades of ivory, cream and white. These classic candles look right in any display, whatever the colours of the flowers or foliage, but don't be afraid to feature them on their own in an all-white arrangement. White candles and flowers are, of course, the traditional way of celebrating many special occasions such as weddings and christenings, but they should not be reserved just for these events. A simple white candle looks perfect on a table in the home or garden, decorated with a few white flowers. Use pale, natural-coloured accessories, perhaps tying the display with a loose bow of raffia or seagrass string. For a larger display, you do not have to have matching candles – a group of white, ivory and cream candles in different shapes and sizes looks very attractive and much less formal. Such a clean, pure and simple look also creates a relaxing and therapeutic setting.

BELOW For an unusual display, group white plaster mouldings with plain, spiralled and moulded candles to echo the shapes and textures of the candles themselves. Any candle display is enhanced if you place a mirror behind it to reflect the candlelight.

The best candles to buy (and the most expensive) are creamy white church (ivory pillar) candles. These contain a proportion of natural beeswax and will therefore burn down more slowly in a display than normal paraffin wax candles. The beeswax gives these candles a lovely pale sheen and a faint smell of honey.

BELOW Shades of cream, gold, ivory and white look beautiful together. Different patterns and textures in the white candlesticks, bowls and plates add detail and interest to this simple display.

ABOVE This delightful summer chandelier is made entirely of white shells. The large scallop shells at the top hold nightlights (tea-lights) and smaller shells are threaded underneath, graduating in size, with a decorative shell at the bottom, which also gives the display some extra weight.

RIGHT For a traditional wedding reception you need a dramatic selection of large white candles and these thick church (ivory pillar) candles will burn for hours. The ridged candles are set on squares of marble, which gives them an attractive air of classic elegance, particularly next to a special, lavish flower display.

S U N N Y
yellow

Spring displays featuring the first fresh flowers of the year would not be the same without bright yellow candles to accentuate the cheerful yellow of daffodils and jasmine, and to contrast vividly with the brilliant green of spring foliage. Combine these elements to create a special and refreshing Easter arrangement. During the summer, candles in all shades of yellow are perfect around the home, at parties and for outdoor entertaining. Go for pale, pretty yellow candles decorated with delicate, dried flowers or the irresistible bold yellow of large sunflowers.

The natural colours and textures of wheat, rope and wood also combine with yellow candles in lovely country candle pots and simple table displays. Yellow candles also look very fresh with white – either with fresh summer daisies or elegant white lilies, and with crisp, clean table linen. The combination of yellow candles, white flowers and green foliage always makes an attractive display for any occasion.

ABOVE This unusual fish candleholder is made out of a large golden-yellow squash, decorated with a lino-cutting tool (linoleum knife) and with holes cut out for small candles that are matching in colour. It is certain to be the focus of attention at an outdoor party. Use scented candles if possible, to fill the garden with a sweet aroma of flowers or incense.

RIGHT As a delightful autumn decoration, use small apples as natural candleholders, making sure that they have quite a sturdy base and will not fall over and spill hot wax. Choose candles in shades of yellow and orange to echo the rich colours of the harvest fields and the falling leaves.

LEFT Beeswax candles need no other embellishment than a ribbon bow in order to look and smell beautiful since they are so stunning in themselves. Their rich golden colour and honeycomb texture is completely natural and of pure quality.

Later in the year, use deep orange or beeswax candles, which make ideal partners for pumpkins, squashes, russet apples and rich-coloured falling leaves. The natural colour of beeswax is a dark, honey yellow, from which traditional rolled candles have been made for centuries. These lovely candles smell deliciously sweet and often have a honeycomb texture that is very attractive in country-style candle pots, reminding us of warm summer days all year round. Their rich texture adds an air of extravagance wherever they are used.

RIGHT Golden oil looks beautifully rich in clear glass oil lamps, especially if you group different shapes and tones together to make a display. Place a golden-yellow oil lamp in the bathroom amongst glass bottles of bath oil and perfume, and add a few drips of lavender or other essential oils, if you like, to create a truly relaxing setting.

DRAMATIC
red

Red is such a popular colour for candles that we are inclined to neglect its full potential. Bright red is an enormously powerful colour, and it is very effective used sparingly to create an impact. Place a scarlet candle with another vivid colour, using for example some lime-green foliage or a stark, black metal candleholder. Used boldly, a red candle can be manipulated in a very simple way to achieve something stunning.

Holly-red candles are traditional at Christmas but for a change try deep burgundy-red candles, which look very handsome against dark evergreens. Each shade of red, from pale pink through to maroon, has quite a different mood suitable for different occasions, so it is worth experimenting with the vibrant range of colours now available.

Match a particular red candle to the colour of an autumn leaf or flower, so that this strong colour merges in with the rest of the design.

Above all, red symbolizes hospitality and a warm welcome, which is why it is so popular for entertaining. Red candles have a deep glow, which is invaluable for creating an intimate atmosphere at any social gathering. Red is also, of course, the traditional colour of love and romance, and a specially decorated luscious red candle or candle box makes a lovely Valentine's Day gift.

LEFT Create a romantic atmosphere with rich red and deep pink candles scented with sensuous fragrances. You can easily mix different candles together for any display.

ABOVE A glowing red pumpkin makes a wonderful decoration, symbolizing warmth and hospitality, especially at Hallowe'en. The folk art patterns carved into the sides of the pumpkin allow the light to shine through, and they can be used to exhibit designs that are highly personalized or perhaps thematic.

LEFT For a glorious autumn table, decorate the base of an orange candle with plumes of brightly coloured red leaves, tied in place with natural raffia. Use it in the garden on still, warm September evenings. Remember to extinguish the candle before the flame reaches the leaves.

TRUE blue

The spectrum of blue candles ranges from cool ice blue to delicate mauve and rich purple, all of which are popular candle colours. Pale blue candles are very fresh in summer and reflect the colours of the sky, while in winter they make an original alternative to a traditional Christmas display. Mix them with other frosted materials, such as wispy seed heads sprayed silver, or with shiny silver baubles.

All shades of blue and mauve are ideal for a lavender candle pot, and the effect is intensified if you add lavender essential oil to scent the candle. Vivid turquoise candles look best in strong sunlight, placed in simple settings reminiscent of Greek islands, or in exotic candleholders. Blue is the colour of the sea, so it is the natural colour to choose for picnics on the beach. Blue and white together always have a jaunty marine look, even if you are only sailing in your imagination. In contrast, midnight blue and purple candles are very much night colours, setting a scene of mystery at your dinner table. These candles need to be used in the dark, with just a flickering pool of light around the table.

BELOW Create an exotic Moroccan-style table by mixing several shades of rich blue together. The vivid turquoise candles provide an extra colour, but make sure the flames do not touch the sides of the cane bird cage.

ABOVE Purple candles combine very successfully with the dark silvery tones of tin candlesticks and lanterns. Vary your candle displays by grouping candles and objects connected by a strong colour theme.

LEFT Midnight blue and pale blue candles create an atmospheric late-night mood. The cool blue colours are enhanced by the clear, watery effect of modern glass candlesticks and an opulent beaded candle collar. Place nightlights (tea-lights) at the base of tall candlesticks to fill a display.

RIGHT You do not always have to colour-match candles to create a pleasing display. Here the rich purple-blue of dried lavender and the soft blue of traditional blue-and-white china is complemented by a pale turquoise candle. Such a rustic look is always popular, and it is very easy to achieve.

green

Whatever flowers and foliage you are using for a display, there is almost certainly a green candle to complement the colour of the leaves. The match does not need to be perfect as different shades of green naturally work well together, but aim for a green that blends in with the whole display. The colours of candles are so realistic that apple- and pear-shaped candles often cannot be distinguished from the real thing.

Pale green and bright emerald-green candles are always happily partnered with white flowers or with a simple white china candleholder for a very crisp, fresh effect. Green candles and white table linen are natural partners, and they are effectively contrasted with either plain linen or lace-edged napkins and tablecloth. Darker green candles have a more rustic feel and combine well with glossy herbs such as bay leaves or oregano in a candle pot that will sit well in the kitchen. They also look very exotic combined with gold, either stencilled on the candle itself or in a gold candleholder or arrangement. At Christmas, green candles appear centre stage with holly and ivy in traditional red and green displays, and also in elegant modern designs of green, ivory and gold. Try to experiment with some of the more unusual shades of green during each season, to surprise your guests and also yourself with what you can achieve.

BELOW A dark forest-green candle in an ornate gold candleholder gives a rich, opulent effect. Use dark green candles at Christmas with abundant displays of glossy green ivy and evergreens, contrasted with a few touches of gold.

RIGHT Decorate a summer table with green glass nightlight (tea-light) holders then pick up the theme with other shades of green. A green party table is perfect in the garden or you can bring the colours of nature indoors.

RIGHT Nothing is more luxurious than having a candle in the bathroom to help you relax and feel pampered. This large marbled candle will burn slowly, and the textures of the green wax, the soap, the smooth glass bowl and the shell soap dish harmonize beautifully for a pure and simple look.

BELOW Another shade of green creates quite a different mood in this pretty flower candleholder. Glass pebbles in water, either plain or coloured, reflect the shimmering candlelight and are an attractive ingredient in a candle display.

T U T T I frutti

Candles are available in every conceivable colour and in all shapes and sizes. Some of the bright waxy colours such as shocking pink and banana yellow have a candy-coated look that makes them almost good enough to eat, while other candle colours are very subtle with several different colours sometimes combined in one candle.

During the making process, candles can be moulded, marbled and decorated in an endless variety of ways to produce multi-coloured designs that are a long way from the traditional idea of a candle. Make the most of this wealth of candle wax, selecting specific candles for occasions such as a child's birthday or a garden party or have fun decorating them yourself. Choose a theme for your candles as you might for fancy dress so that they work together well. The beauty of candles is that you can create a magic, glowing world for one evening, then replace it on the next occasion with something new.

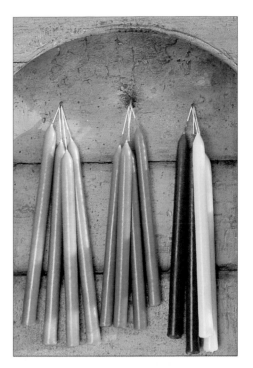

ABOVE Traditional dipped candles look decorative simply hanging from a nail on the wall to dry. You can dip them repeatedly to achieve a solid colour, or make white candles and overdip them with a coat of coloured wax. Coated candles have a more intense colour than solid-colour candles and they are less likely to fade.

ABOVE Hand-painted candles decorated with simple spots and stripes are the perfect party accessory. Here gold paint turns plain white and red candles into something special and you can experiment with other colours.

RIGHT Candle wax dyes produce intense colours in a dazzling range of shades. Burnt orange, purple and dark red are just a few of the rich colours available, shown here in star-shaped pyramid and pillar candles. Shaped candles are also easily made as there is a wide range of moulds available.

LEFT These brightly patterned ceramic candlesticks call for candles in vivid colours such as lime green and scarlet. Ring the changes by choosing a different colour when you replace a candle, to create a new look for your table or when entertaining. They are just right for a celebratory atmosphere.

CANDLES FOR ALL

seasons

■ ■ ■ ■

Decorating with candles is an excellent way to make the most of each season, quickly and simply changing your decor to follow the colours of nature. Bring woodland materials and fresh flowers indoors and incorporate them in your candle designs to give them character.

SIGNS OF
spring

The first delicate primroses and narcissi of the year are a wonderful excuse to brighten up your home with spring-coloured candles and fresh flowers. Yellow and green candles are associated especially with this season, either in pale, delicate shades or bright, cheerful colours, depending on the flowers you choose to accompany them. Branches of buds and early flowers such as forsythia and pussy willow, appear in gardens and along riverbanks, creating an opportunity for larger displays with tall beeswax candles. By

Easter, there are plenty of yellow and white spring flowers to combine with candles for a table centrepiece, or an individual display around the base of a candlestick. Pastel candles also suit the delicate character of springtime, and a good source of inspiration is the subtle colour of birds' eggs. Stronger blue candles complement the intense blue of flowers such as grape hyacinths.

For more informal entertaining, egg-shaped candles in realistic colours will make witty Easter decorations, and guests will be enchanted by the gift of a candle pot or candle box specially made for the occasion.

LEFT Complement the beautiful creamy colour of a thick church (ivory pillar) candle with an exuberant plume of parrot tulip petals around the base. This stunning display will certainly let your guests know that spring has finally arrived.

BELOW Frothy spring blossom and cream candles make a lovely delicate display. Vary the size and height of the candles to add interest to the simple grouping. Choose the palest candles and flowers to add just a few hints of pastel colour.

ABOVE Egg-shaped candles are subtly coloured to look just like the real thing. Incorporate them in an Easter display or place them in little baskets or egg boxes as charming gifts for your guests.

BELOW Yellow flowers and green foliage create a classic spring bouquet in a pedestal candlestick. Beehive candles are rolled round here into a hive-shaped dome.

LONG
summer days

Summer is the time for entertaining outside on the patio or in the garden, with the soft, atmospheric glow of candlelight taking over as the sun's rays begin to fade. There are many ways to decorate with candles outdoors, varying from tin lanterns and flower border lamps to pretty, sweet-scented table displays. Terracotta flowerpots make excellent summer candleholders, for use indoors or out. If you are using them in the garden, mix them in with similar pots full of flowering plants to make an instant display.

Use colourful fresh or dried flowers to decorate the base of a candle, or to create a larger centrepiece for a table. Vivid reds, pinks and yellows look good in strong sunlight or you may prefer pastel pinks and mauves, depending on your mood as well as the occasion. The nice thing about candles is that you can quickly and easily create a different display from one day to the next.

Herbs are very popular displayed with candles, both for their soft green colours and for their aromatic scent. You often need a mass of herbs to achieve an effect, but they are in plentiful supply at this time of year, and look at their best when they are a glossy, healthy green colour. Lavender is a favourite for decorating or scenting a candle, and its strong aroma, released by the flame of the candle, may deter unwelcome insects when you are eating outdoors. For the best setting of all for a meal, take simple blue and white candles with you to the beach for an impromptu gathering around a driftwood fire. Soft candlelight on a warm summer night by the sea is sure to create a magical atmosphere that will be unforgettable.

LEFT Four tall and thin coloured candles look very effective simply positioned on one side of a ring of elegant, mixed summer flowers. Choose candle colours that will pick out and accentuate the colours of the flowers in the ring. Remember to extinguish candles before they reach any materials used on flower and other displays.

ABOVE These bold tulip candlesticks are ornamental enough to stand on their own or to use with a lavish display of summer blooms for more formal entertaining. It is worth having one or two decorative candleholders such as this to use on occasion as the mood suits you.

BELOW This simple arrangement of intensely coloured flowers is low enough to sit in the centre of a table without being in the way. The alternating height of the candles gives the design an attractive shape. It is an ideal display for evening dinner or afternoon tea, or may be simply placed on a mantelpiece.

ABOVE Pink and blue dried flowers make a romantic candle decoration for summer evenings in the garden. Add a little sweet-scented oil to accentuate the perfume of the roses, if you like. The base is simply made up of a bag of sand covered in fabric and tied with a ribbon bow.

HARVEST time

As the long evenings begin to draw in, we spend more time indoors, returning home to the welcome of a fire and the warm glow of candlelight. This is the season of warm, ruddy colours, ripe sheaves of wheat and abundant fruit in the fields and orchards, and glistening berries in the hedgerows. To tone in with the season's colours, choose fat candles in oranges, reds and cinnamon browns and use some of the ripe fruits and berries to decorate candle pots and to make rich, colourful displays.

Giant orange pumpkins with grinning Jack o' Lantern faces are well known for Hallowe'en, but you can also use small, green-striped squash and many other varieties to hold candles or nightlights (tea-lights). Wheat and barley should not be overlooked – they make lovely natural country displays, teamed with terracotta flowerpots and cream church (ivory pillar) candles and you often find them growing wild in the countryside. This is the time of year to collect dried poppy seed heads, pine cones and attractive grasses to use now or in winter arrangements. Meanwhile, make the most of the russet and yellow falling leaves, saving large ones to wrap around candles or candle boxes.

BELOW This highly original display combines pale yellow roses with a small, creamy-yellow squash to make a glorious centrepiece for an autumn table. The gold-brown candle is the perfect finishing touch.

ABOVE Neutral colours echo the mood of the dry brown leaves at this time of year. A lantern is a welcome sight hanging outside the front door as the autumn evenings begin to turn chilly and damp. Choose other decorations and accessories, such as shaped holders and picture frames, to continue the leaf theme and its deep colours.

ABOVE RIGHT Glass nightlight (tea-light) holders come in rich colours, and you can choose some that will match the autumn leaves and hang them from a tree in the garden. Suspend them from the wire around the top or group them indoors on a wide windowsill or shelf. The flame is well protected inside the glass container, but do make sure that there are no leaves blocking off the top of the holder or falling inside, as they may be a fire hazard. Nightlights burn for a good few hours and are easily replaced, so it is certainly worth the time spent erecting the display.

RIGHT Rich golden pumpkin lanterns are traditional at Hallowe'en and these little candleholders are a charming variation. Simply choose pumpkins that stand quite sturdily and hollow out the top to fit a candle in snugly. Orange and yellow candles continue the autumn theme.

cheer

During the long days indoors, the bright, cheerful light of candles is especially welcome. Simple candle pots decorated with nuts or dried flowers are ideal for everyday use, and it is always nice to welcome your guests with a candle lantern outside the front door.

For dinners and parties, candle-lit chandeliers and candelabra have an impressive, magical effect that will entrance your guests. They look very opulent, but you can make your own modern-style candelabra or chandelier out of very basic materials. Towards the end of the year, candle displays with evergreens such as blue pine and bay leaves bring nature indoors to remind us that the bushes will be green again in the spring.

BELOW Welcome guests to your home at Christmas with a small terracotta candle pot, protected from the elements by a heavy cast iron lantern. Decorate the wall around the lantern with dried twigs, and add a floppy fabric bow made from ornate material.

RIGHT Creamy church (ivory pillar) candles harmonize with weathered terracotta flowerpots and natural woodland materials for a winter decoration. Collect nuts, pine cones, twigs and moss, and glue them round the top of the pot to make a collar.

The height of the candle year is
Christmas, with all its symbolic
associations. Rich red and green candles
combined with holly and ivy are, of
course, traditional at Christmas, but pale
candles such as ivory, cream, silver and
gold are a very attractive modern
alternative. The candles on the Victorian
Christmas tree have been replaced by
fairy (electric) lights, but we can re-
create the fairytale world of twinkling
lights by surrounding the candlelight
with faceted glass, silver or metal.
Another idea for a Christmas display is to
drape the mantelpiece with a lavish swag
made up of different materials, often
evergreens, and decorated with gilded or
frosted candle pots.

ABOVE For an attractive gift or decoration
make a still life in a hessian-covered
cardboard box. Mix dried flowers and fungi
with seashells and a large church (ivory
pillar) candle that will burn down slowly.
Allow some of the materials to hang over the
sides of the box to give a full, overflowing
effect, and use reindeer moss to fill any gaps.
Dried flowers and spices such as cinnamon
sticks will add a faint sweet-scented aroma.
This attractive display is ideally suited to a
bathroom setting, but try to keep the bottom
of the box completely dry.

LEFT A cheerful red candle in a brass lantern
symbolizes warmth and hospitality even on
the coldest winter day. The outline of a gold
star painted on the glass accentuates the
flickering candle flame. Use it outside to
contrast against crisp white snow, or display
it inside on a window sill to create a
welcoming warm glow for all to see.

themes

■ ■ ■ ■

When you are decorating your home or entertaining, it often helps to
have a specific theme on which you can work. Candles create
atmosphere and can be used to help conjure up many different effects
such as mysterious, witty, rustic or nostalgic.

SEASIDE
memories

We all remember sunny days on the beach spent collecting shells, pebbles and nuggets of cloudy glass or rough pieces of bleached driftwood and weathered rope. These beachcombing treasures can be made into delightful candleholders to add light to a beach barbecue, or to bring back home and remind us of the sea. Shells make wonderful natural containers for candle wax, and shell candles are very easy to make at home. The exterior of such shells is often fantastically patterned, but the inside is a delicate pearly pink, which shimmers beautifully in the light of the candle. Continue the seaside theme by supporting the shell candles in sand and surrounding them with a range of decorative, small shells, starfish and smooth, round pebbles.

Small moulded fish shapes are perfect floating candles, especially if you keep your colours to royal blue and white. A bowl of floating fish candles would be the ideal centrepiece for a buffet with a seaside theme, surrounded by other marine materials.

The natural place for seaside candles is in the bathroom, where the steamy conditions suit shells and pebbles perfectly. Place your candles on the window sill and dream of sailing away in a driftwood boat with a candle mast.

BELOW A large, rugged shell is a perfect natural container for candle wax, surrounded by other seaside mementos. Shell candles look at home resting in sand, which is moulded around them to give them support.

ABOVE The fascinating texture of oyster shells contrasts beautifully with smooth cream candle wax. These lovely candles would be perfect for a summer party. They are easy to make, and the shells can be re-filled with wax and a new wick when the candle burns down.

ABOVE RIGHT For a witty trompe l'oeil effect, present a group of shell-shaped moulded candles in a box of sand. The opaque texture of wax perfectly imitates the pearly surface of the sea shells, and they can burn until the flame reaches the sand. Many different designs are available from specialist suppliers.

RIGHT Decorate a seaside table with a shell candle pot. The terracotta flowerpot is covered with fringed hessian, which is held in place by string threaded through a large shell. Extra shells surround the large candle to fill any gaps.

COUNTRY style

This is the most popular decorating style, and one of the easiest to achieve. Look out for rustic textures such as weathered terracotta flowerpots, tin cans, rope and driftwood, and recycle them into attractive candle pots and boxes, and even candelabra. Decorate the candleholders with natural materials such as dried wheat and barley, grasses, poppy seed heads and pine cones, found growing wild in the fields and woods on country walks and display your candle on a blue-and-white checkered tablecloth.

Dried flowers are an important ingredient in country-style displays, often teamed with a cream church (ivory pillar) candle for a very simple look. Dried lavender, herbs and rosebuds are especially popular in scented candle pots and candle collars, recalling the colours and perfumes of an old-fashioned cottage garden. Tie these simple displays with natural raffia as the ideal finishing touch. Honey-scented beeswax candles are very much at home with this style; they have been made in the same traditional way for centuries and are completely natural. Try making them yourself, to the size and shape that is suited to your requirements.

More inspiration for country style comes from Central Europe, where wooden candlesticks are often painted with stylized folk art motifs in rich earthy colours and candles are stencilled with simple repetitive patterns and traditional designs. Tin lanterns and collars are also popular in many cultures and are very practical as the candle flame is enclosed and protected within them. The soft tin can easily be punched with holes so that the candlelight shines through in a delicate, decorative pattern.

LEFT This charming blue-and-white china candlestick, decorated with a stylized plant motif, epitomizes the country look. Natural fabrics, gingham checks, wicker baskets, wood, raffia and wax candles work well together to create a calm, soothing environment that never goes out of fashion.

BELOW Turned wooden candlesticks always look right, whether or not they are painted or left as natural wood. It is easy to add interesting-looking signs of wear and tear by rubbing the paintwork back in places.

ABOVE Simple lavender candle collars tied with narrow ribbon bows give these barley-twist candles the flavour of the French countryside. The mauve candles are moulded in the shape of lavender bundles and are made from lavender-scented wax.

RIGHT A rustic metal candelabra gives instant style and grace to a table. Old candelabra can sometimes be found in junk shops and restored, but always remember to leave a slightly distressed appearance for true country style. Plain white candles are the best to use for such a style. It is easy to find any size to fit different types of holders.

WAXY fruits

Fruit candles are so realistic that they are almost indistinguishable from the real thing and are often placed alongside real fruit in a fruit bowl. They are made in plastic, glass, metal or rubber moulds, which can be used over and over again to produce a batch of identical fruits. Adding a suitable fruity or citrus scent to the wax makes the candles even more attractive when you finally have the heart to light them. Attach a few leaves for extra authenticity if you wish and paint the wick dark brown to look like the fruit's natural stalk. Candles imitating soft fruits such as colourful strawberries and peaches are popular, but the favourite fruit candles are apples, pears, lemons and oranges, because their waxy texture is so much like the real fruit. They look especially attractive in autumn with dark orange pumpkin lanterns in a display of harvest produce.

You can also use real apples as candleholders – cut a slice off the base so that the apple is stable and then hollow out the top with an apple corer to hold a nightlight (tea-light) or candle stub. Small squash can be treated in the same way to make lovely little holders, especially if you use one of the decorative green-striped varieties.

BELOW Waxy pear candles look very realistic, especially when placed among real fruit such as these red apples. Even little marks and blemishes are detailed on the wax surface. Many fruit candles are also scented with an appropriate perfume.

BELOW A group of fruit candles on a glass plate provides a source of low light in the centre of a dinner table. Each of these pears is equipped with a leaf as well as a realistic brown stalk, which is of course the wick. They would make an ideal romantic display to accompany a sensuous meal.

RIGHT This dish of mixed candle fruits would make a lovely decoration for a Christmas table, providing an inventive and attractive alternative to the traditional bowl of fresh fruit. Alternatively, place the wax orange at the bottom of a Christmas stocking for a trompe l'oeil surprise. Light them and bring them to the table with dessert, coffee and liqueurs as the natural light outside slowly begins to fade.

F L O W E R
garden

Fresh and dried flowers are natural partners to candles, but when the flowers in question are themselves candles, the effect is magical. These little novelties always attract attention at a buffet or party, especially if you place them in miniature terracotta flowerpots or among real flowers. During the summer, they create a delightful effect in the early evening, dotted among plants in a flower border or windowbox so that individual points of candlelight begin to twinkle as the sunlight fades. A large glass bowl of floating flower candles is a lovely way to decorate a table, and you can relax in the knowledge that this is a very safe way to display candles. The wavering light from the tiny candles is gloriously reflected by the water, and you can increase the magical effect by positioning wine glasses nearby so that they also reflect the candlelight.

A beautiful, delicate way to combine candles and flowers is with hand-pressed flowers, which can be invisibly held in place on a candle by a thin layer of melted wax. Sweet-scented flowers such as lavender and roses are traditionally associated with candles as symbols of romance or as "tokens of affection". A gift of flowers and candles is always welcome, especially if you have assembled it yourself.

ABOVE For a quick and easy party decoration, float pretty flower candles in a glass bowl of water and add toning petals and leaves. Surround the bowl with candles in coloured glass containers and masses of different flowers.

RIGHT Novelty candles include these colourful baskets of flowers and many floating flowers. Place them in amongst vivid blooms to surprise and delight your guests at a summer party in the garden. Light the candles as the daylight fades.

ABOVE For a special gift, press or dry the pretty little "faces" of pansy flowers and use them to decorate the sides of a cream or pastel-coloured candle. Add layers of ribbons for a lovely old-world effect. These will of course be all the more irresistible if a few drips of scented oil are added to the wax. Display strewn with a layer of deeply coloured soft single petals.

RIGHT Float flower-shaped candles in a large glass bowl or in individual glass tumblers, adding whole flower heads and petals to co-ordinate with the colours. Coloured glass makes the watery reflections even more entrancing. Floating candles are easy to make, and there are many different types of moulds available according to the type of flower head you wish to make.

C O S M I C
symbols

Our fascination with light dates back to our earliest ancestry, when many people worshipped the sun. The Inca civilization used pure gold to symbolize its golden-yellow colour, and today the skies still exert a powerful force over our imaginations.

Real gold suns, moons and stars can be transferred directly on to plain candles using the ancient technique of gold leaf, creating magical images that shimmer in the light. Another traditional technique is to stencil cosmic shapes on to the candle, using gold or silver spray paint. The stencil can be used again and again to make a perfect repeat, so you can create a whole constellation of tiny stars. All these shapes are very simple to draw in outline, and can be used to decorate candleholders as well as the candles themselves. Stars are especially associated with Christmas, and this is a good time to combine cosmic candles with other silver and gold accessories in a lavish and festive mantelpiece display, with seasonal fruits such as pomegranates.

One of the many moods you can create with candles is that of mystery, drama and intrigue. Gold and silver suns, moons and stars look lovely on white or cream candles, and give a completely different effect on deep purple or midnight blue candles.

BELOW Stars and suns are popular motifs on candlesticks and candleholders, as they have been for centuries. Fill them with gold and amber candles by day, and with purple and deep blue candles at night. Add extra cosmic motifs and symbolic fruits to make a powerful display.

ABOVE This wooden candlestick has been gilded with aluminium leaf, giving the radiant sun motif enormous power and resonance. The large, squat candle is the perfect accompaniment for such a vibrant base. Display it with complementary bright colours to really make it come alive.

ABOVE Gold-stencilled patterns transform plain cream candles into magical decorations. Gold- or silver-sprayed motifs, such as stars and crescent moons, also look very atmospheric on dark, dramatic colours. Experiment with scarlet or midnight blue.

RIGHT Pile up gilded star shapes to make an impressive stand for a single round gold candle to place in the most important part of the room. The shimmering reflection of the candle flame creates the sense of a mysterious other world.

around the home

■ ■ ■ ■

Choose different candles and candle displays to suit different rooms

and different moods. Don't neglect the kitchen and bathroom, where

aromatic herbs and scented candles can be used as a real treat,

particularly as an accompaniment to a warm, relaxing bath.

IN THE living room

Candles are a lovely way to quickly and easily change the character of a family room, giving it a new look for each season of the year. Refurbish terracotta candle pots with different-coloured candles and matching candle collars, such as a pale mauve candle in the summer with a collar of fresh or dried lavender. In the winter, the same candle pot will look quite different with a cream church (ivory pillar) candle and silver-sprayed nuts or pine cones. Small displays like this are ideal for brightening dark corners and odd angles in a room, where there would not be enough daylight for a vase of fresh flowers.

When you are entertaining, particularly at Christmas, more lavish displays will be needed. Chandeliers are wonderfully romantic and luxurious, and modern versions can be made out of the most unlikely prosaic materials that will intrigue as well as delight your guests. As long as you have a high enough ceiling, this is quite a safe way to feature candles at a party as they cannot be knocked over by mistake.

BELOW The rich colours of the oranges and the wire-edged gold ribbon are echoed by elegant gold candles in a set of matching candlesticks in this aromatic mantelpiece.

ABOVE Tinware candelabra from countries such as Mexico and India are relatively inexpensive compared to antique silver candleholders. Grouped together on a mantelpiece, they make a dazzling display to welcome guests in the evening, particularly if placed above a roaring log fire.

ABOVE LEFT Dress up an old silver candelabra for a special occasion by twining ivy around the branches, then add two white lilies to complement the candles. Placing a candle-lit display in front of a mirror increases its impact. Such a combination makes a well-received display for a wedding reception or a summer gathering.

Bright tin lanterns are also attractive in such settings and are very safe, as the candle or nightlight (tea-light) is protected in an enclosed space. Shiny holders look magical grouped around the edge of a fireplace or on a window sill outlined against the dark winter night, with the curtains left undrawn. The mantelpiece is another surface that lends itself to exotic candle displays, draped with swags of Christmas evergreens or gilded rope. Be as daring and imaginative as you like, and allow the display to dominate the room.

LEFT Metal and wirework are very fashionable and provide unusual, quirky candleholders. It is very effective to arrange several different designs together in a group united by a common theme, such as a particular colour or, as here, a type of material. Place on a table, or if tall enough, allow the holder to stand up alone in the corner of a room or on a patio outside.

IN THE
dining room

Whether the next event on the social calendar is an informal family meal or a grand dinner party, this one room often has to be able to assume different styles and moods within a few hours. In the evening, candlelight will transform it into a magical world full of twinkling cutlery and shimmering wine glasses, even before you begin to add any other decoration. Children's toys may be lurking in the dark corners of the room, but candles help us suspend disbelief and enclose us in a small, warm circle of light cocooned from the everyday world outside. Even when there is no special occasion, sharing a meal by the intimate light of a candle makes us sit and talk instead of rushing off somewhere else. Candleholders, especially those decorated with favourite designs such as folk art motifs, suggest hospitality and warmth and are ideal for relaxing supper parties. Both family and friends will appreciate unusual ideas accompanied with seasonal flowers to decorate the table at different times of year.

If there is no room on the table for a candle, or it would mean stretching over the flame, a good alternative is to place it on a sideboard. This gives more room to display a group of candles that will light the room, so that you can see to eat while retaining the intimate atmosphere. Use collections of jam jars, mismatched china or tin lanterns for everyday meals, and create more theatrical silver or gold displays for formal dinners.

BELOW Candles create an atmosphere even at an informal dining table. Here the ornamental wire fruit basket has three built-in candleholders, and the simple black candelabra is useful for adding height.

RIGHT Whether candles are being used on the dining table at meal times or are positioned on a side table throughout the day, candles will create a focal point of interest in the dining room. These simple, plain candles complement this lavish fruit and flower festive display, yet they have a stately presence of their own, positioned as they are in these tall and elegant, shiny metal candlesticks.

ABOVE An inviting table setting juxtaposes contemporary earthenware with traditional terracotta pots from the garden grouped on a serving plate for a look of understated chic. The candle pots have been specially painted to match the plates at this homely table. Extra light is provided by small weathered flower pots with glowing candle flames inside them, placed on a plate scattered with quail's eggs.

LEFT Create a sumptuous setting with a blue-and-gold brocade tablecloth and braid-edged gold overcloth. Continue the exotic theme and rich colours with brass goblets and plates, brass candlesticks and tall gold candles. Such a display makes any meal a very special occasion.

IN THE kitchen

Country-style pine kitchens are not complete without a terracotta candle pot or wooden candle box decorated with soft green aromatic herbs. In some of these candle displays the bay leaves, bunches of thyme and oregano, garlic heads and chillies can be removed to use in cooking, which is a lovely gift idea for a friend's kitchen. The combination of candlelight, herbs and the scent of home cooking is irresistible, and the perfect way for both you and your guests to look forward to a delicious meal.

In high-tech kitchens, basic white candles are all that is needed, displayed in simple white china candleholders or Shaker-style metal containers. These functional white candles also complement a blue-and-white decor, combined with striped and check fabrics for a very clean, fresh image. For a more decorative look, these simple candles can easily be transformed with hand-painted stripes or a simple motif.

BELOW Beeswax candles and bottled homemade preserves create a lovely inviting atmosphere.

If you have a dining table in the kitchen, an attractive candle centrepiece decorated with fresh or dried flowers will make informal meals seem much more civilized. Choose a small, low display that will not be in the way, and adapt it by adding mini-vegetables or ornamental vegetable leaves, according to season, to make a witty reference to culinary ingredients. Remember that kitchens are also practical places, so they are also an ideal place to exhibit candles that are being stored in decorative boxes wrapped in checkered cloths.

BELOW Store plain white candles ready for use whenever you need them. This traditional wooden candle box is ideal and a piece of blue-and-white check fabric tied with linen tape not only protects them, but also makes the box decorative as well as practical. It is useful to have candles ready-to-hand for when you feel in the mood for candlelight, so the kitchen is an ideal room in which to keep them as it is such a central and key room in any house.

ABOVE These scalloped tin candleholders look best with simple white candles. Their shiny metal surfaces complement wooden tables and accessories, kitchen spoons and saucepans to give a Shaker-style look.

ABOVE RIGHT This utility-style chandelier is made from a galvanized tray suspended from the kitchen ceiling. Glass jam jars filled with nightlights (tea-lights) reflect the light well and will look good resting on shelves too.

IN THE bathroom

The most self-indulgent way to unwind is undoubtedly in a steaming hot bath with a scented candle glowing gently on the window sill. At night, a lavender-scented candle will make you feel relaxed and sleepy, while in the morning a stimulating scent of rosemary will make you feel alert and invigorated. Richer scents will create a lovely romantic or therapeutic atmosphere as you choose. Place the candle amongst a group of colourful glass bottles containing bath oil and perfume, or in front of a mirror, so that the candlelight is magnified and reflected. Small candles or nightlights (tea-lights) in attractive tin containers will sit happily on the end of the bath itself for an intimate feel.

Seashell-covered candleholders are ideal in the bathroom, where the steamy atmosphere will keep the beautifully patterned shells looking as bright and shiny as when you picked them up on the beach. The moist bathroom atmosphere, however, isn't at all suitable for candle pots containing dried flowers, pine cones or seed heads, which need to be kept dry. Continue the seaside theme with glass jars of pebbles, nuggets of sea-clouded glass and a candleholder boat made out of a piece of driftwood with seagrass string for rigging. Alternatively, if your bathroom decor is predominantly a simple white, you could choose marine blue and white candles for a very jaunty look. The bathroom, after all, is a place to dream and plan your holidays, so use lots of candles and allow your imagination to run wild.

ABOVE An ornate candelabra can be as much at home in the bathroom as in the living or dining room. Its elegance will certainly make taking a bath something of an occasion, and the flickering candlelight is very therapeutic.

RIGHT Place candles on the window sill amongst coloured and patterned glass bottles of bath oil and perfume so that the candlelight creates magical shafts of coloured light. A mirror and other shiny metallic surfaces will reflect the shimmering light and magnify the effect.

ABOVE Amuse family and guests, as well as yourself, with tiny metal candleholders, some shaped like boats, dotted around the bathroom. Place them randomly on different available surfaces to give them extra height and added interest. Large, square candles imitate the waxy texture of French blocks of soap, making a particularly nice feature.

RIGHT Create a beautiful dressing-table area with a scallop shell candle and bottles of luxurious bath oil. The soft candlelight is the perfect atmosphere when you are preparing for a special evening or to bathe as part of your everyday routine in a romantic and relaxing glow.

IN THE bedroom

Small candles are very attractive in the bedroom, especially if you match the colours of the candle and display to the predominant colour in your curtains and bedlinen. Country-style candle pots and small displays are ideal, decorated with pretty dried flowers and tied with ribbon. A pink or red candle surrounded by a collar of roses or tiny rosebuds will create a romantic mood, which you can accentuate by scenting the candle with a few drops of your favourite essential oil. Sweet-scented lavender with a pale mauve, blue or purple candle is soothing and restful. Lavender was traditionally used by housewives to scent their linen cupboards, and it is still popular today in herbal pillows to induce sleep. In a guest bedroom, a small posy of fresh flowers with a candle in the centre is very welcoming and thoughtful. If the candle display is expected to last only one or two days, you can choose delicate short-lived flowers as these are often the prettiest.

Particularly in the bedroom, there is a danger of falling asleep while the candle is still lit, so it is a wise precaution to use enclosed candleholders and small, stable candles. Place the candle on a safe surface away from the side of the bed, such as an uncurtained window sill or small table and do not leave any burning candles unattended.

BELOW A simple candle makes beautiful patterns of light in a group of glass containers with silver lids, giving a soft, soothing effect. The bowl candleholder becomes a pool of light.

ABOVE Use different-coloured candles to create different moods. Here, the more unusual hues of the rich golden-brown candles have a very earthy and relaxing effect. Grouping candles of the same colour together adds to their impact. The candles are complemented by seasonal flowers in a very simple display.

ABOVE RIGHT A clear glass container is all that is required for a romantic boudoir as the colour is provided by the seductive fabrics, heart-shaped perfume bottles and pillow, and the sparkling jewellery. The candlelight brings these various elements to life and really seals the sensuous atmosphere.

RIGHT A metal wall sconce is very practical in a bedroom as well as extremely decorative. This scalloped sconce, decorated with a stylized flower motif, is ideal in a country-style bedroom with stencilled walls and a patchwork quilt. The circular blue holder also makes a rustic lantern and is a safe way of using candles in the bedroom.

IN THE
garden

Magazines and television programmes have taught us to think of the garden or patio as another room, which we can decorate with different colours and textures. In the evening, candles transform the well-known plants and bushes of daylight into a different, fairytale world. Rustic candleholders such as terracotta flowerpots or small metal buckets look at home in the garden, and will withstand any frosts overnight. Lanterns of all kinds also fit in with the outdoor theme and can be suspended very attractively from the branch of a tree. Whatever the candlelight falls on will be magically illuminated while the rest of the garden is in darkness. If you only have a very limited space, even a windowbox, place flower-shaped candles among your plants for maximum effect – they will be well noticed here, whereas they might be lost in a larger space.

For informal meals in the daytime, place an unlit candle on a pretty saucer or candleholder and decorate it with flowers or herbs picked straight from the garden. Add a bow of natural raffia for the perfect finishing touch. As the sun sets and the light gradually fades, you can light the candle that you have already enjoyed by daylight. At dusk, when insects are often a nuisance, a burning candle scented with lavender or citronella essential oils will keep any small pests away.

BELOW For an unusual garden decoration, pick vegetable leaves and tie them around candles with raffia. Add attractive vegetables such as runner beans and radishes, or whatever is available in season. Fit small candles into seedpods such as horse chestnuts to make improvized candleholders.

ABOVE Even on still summer evenings, it is as well to protect outdoor lights in case they blow out in a sudden gust of wind. Lanterns are ideal as the flame is completely enclosed, and they can be hung from available supports. Position them around various attractive objects in the garden, such as old vases and weathered watering cans that have been filled with branches of leaves, for a very attractive garden display.

ABOVE RIGHT An outdoor chandelier is a lovely idea, particularly at Christmas. This version is an ornamental wirework basket with candleholders around the top, filled with large pine cones and variegated holly. Simple white candles are all that is needed to put a finishing touch to this display.

RIGHT Gilded terracotta flowerpots look gorgeous filled with rich yellow wax that radiates the candlelight. Place a group low down on the ground amongst the garden plants and surround them with large pebbles, and they will give the impression of a pathway of light twirling around the garden.

with candles

■ ■ ■ ■

Parties are the time to be theatrical. Indulge yourself and your guests

with wonderful candle creations made in rich, exotic colours. The

magical setting suggested by candlelight provides an experience that

will seem like an enchanting dream the next day.

DINNER parties

This is the ultimate opportunity to create a beautiful setting with romantic, atmospheric candlelight. Entertaining begins when guests arrive and are offered a pre-dinner drink, so it is a good idea to introduce the candlelit theme with single candlesticks or small displays on occasional tables and sideboards. When you enter the dining room, a traditional pair of tall, majestic candlesticks at either end of a long table looks impressive. A candelabra, traditional or modern, in the centre of the table gives the same grand effect, and slim, tapered candles suit these elegant candleholders.

This is also the time to experiment with mood-creating colours such as midnight blue or deep amber-yellow. A lavish display in the centre of the dinner table might mix candles with luscious fruit and flowers, to stimulate the tastebuds as well as enchant the eye. A modern alternative is witty candle designs with food connotations, "served" on plates, which are certain to be an unusual talking point. After dinner, when you return to the living room, co-ordinate the candle colours with tempting displays of beautifully wrapped chocolates to create decorations that are good enough to eat.

ABOVE Delight your guests with tiny fishing-boat candles made out of mussel shells filled with plain wax. The inside of the black shells changes from blue to mauve to purple in the flickering light of the little flames. They make a delicious-looking display that celebrates the joy of eating and encourages a hungry appetite, making the food around the table even more appealing.

RIGHT A dramatic combination of colours makes a dinner table look stunning without going to great expense. Here bright emerald green glass candlesticks and china are beautifully set off by the soft, luscious texture of rich red strawberries and roses for a delicious, mouth-watering display.

ABOVE For a formal Christmas dinner, pile the table with abundance. A classic candelabra looks magnificent with gold candles, and four staggered beeswax candles echo the pale flowers in a low arrangement. Now is the time to display waxy fruit candles in the fruit bowl, flower-shaped candles below a vase and tiny nightlights (tea-lights) to fill any empty spaces.

RIGHT Prepare a witty first course out of artichoke leaves tied to a large candle with raffia, and present it on the plate with complementing red and green salad leaves. Your guests can take the artichoke candles home as novel gifts afterwards, if they like.

G A R D E N
parties

Celebrate long summer evenings by entertaining outdoors whenever possible. Place small candles and lanterns at different heights, suspending some of the lanterns from trees, to create an enchanted secret garden with hidden corners. The candleholders will not be visible in the dark so you can use simple glass jam jars or tin cans. Start collecting the decorative glass dishes that can often be found in junkshops as their faceted surfaces reflect the light beautifully and they cost next to nothing.

BELOW Create a colourful table for an informal summer party outdoors with fruit, flowers and candles. The glass containers will protect the candle flames if there is any wind, and also prevent guests touching the flames if they stretch over the table.

If you have a garden path or a path leading to the front door, it is a lovely idea to place these glass candleholders on either side to direct your guests, and also to welcome them as they arrive. Decorate the tables where you will be serving food and drinks with plenty of candles as they will be the only source of light later in the evening. Wine glasses and bottles will magnify the candlelight, and a display of seasonal fruits such as strawberries or cherries will appear even more intensely red. For a formal party, you may prefer a traditional approach, for example, silver candelabra or candlesticks with white candles and frosted green grapes piled high on an elegant glass dish. An outdoor chandelier lit by small candles will enchant everyone, and you can make a very simple one out of natural woodland materials. Decorate it for the evening with trailing ivy or gold cord, giving it a different look for each occasion.

ABOVE Some empty tin cans from the kitchen are very decorative and are too good to throw away, so recycle them as colourful containers for candle wax. The metal surface of the tins reflects the candlelight, especially as the wax burns down.

ABOVE RIGHT Collect baroque-style candles and candleholders ready for a party. Scarlet and gold candles decorated with stars or embossed with fake jewels set the theme, and the pewter candelabra, candlestick and miniature crown holders complete the embellished image.

RIGHT Inexpensive embossed glass tumblers and jam jars make magical containers for candles and nightlights (tea-lights). Placing a silver tray underneath them reflects and fragments the light and adds an extra sparkle and richness.

SPECIAL celebrations

The great social events of our lives are closely associated with candles, which have come to symbolize celebrations and festivities of all kinds. White candles look beautiful at weddings and christenings, and appropriate-coloured candles mark anniversaries such as a golden wedding. For such important occasions, a lovely idea is to design your own set of matching candles stencilled with a simple repeated pattern in gold or silver for a really special effect. Candles for children can feature cartoon characters and all kinds of fun pictures and designs to suit their personal favourite ideas.

Birthdays are great fun because you can design a cake or display based on any theme, and make full use of the colourful and novelty candles now available. Easter is another occasion to use brightly coloured candles, either egg-yolk yellow or primary colours inspired by folk art. Pale yellow candles with yellow and white spring flowers create quite a different effect – choose a new display each year, depending on the age of your family and guests.

Hallowe'en is a lovely celebration for candle-lovers, with rich, warm candlelight glowing through orange pumpkin faces. Experiment with other squashes, then group them all together on a party table. Christmas, of course, is the main celebration of the year in which candles play a leading role. Follow the traditional colour theme of red and green candles in evergreen swags and displays, choose frosted and gilded candles with silver and gold accessories or create your own celebratory look.

LEFT Ring the changes on the traditional Hallowe'en pumpkin lantern by experimenting with different shapes and colours. Gourds, squashes and even swedes can be carved into the most fantastic geometric or ornate patterns. Their warm glow will be irresistible.

BELOW A mix-and-match group of inexpensive aluminium candlesticks is exactly right for a christening. Plain white candles are all that are needed, with silvery grey and white ribbon bows.

RIGHT Painted eggs are traditional in many countries of Eastern Europe, and these decorative egg candles are in the same tradition. You can also make egg candles yourself using egg-shaped moulds that split in half to release the candle when the wax has set. They would make lovely gifts for friends and family at Easter.

LEFT A short, thick candle has been painted gold to make an ideal Christmas display. The small, delicate holly-shaped leaves are also made out of wax and alternate between gold and green for a very festive look and colour.

FAR LEFT Decorate a home-made birthday cake with brightly coloured twisted candles set in hand-painted flower holders. Complete the table with red and yellow flowers and Chinese lanterns, and a "bouquet" of pretty little flower candles.

candles

■ ■ ■ ■

There are certain times when you want something extra-special, for a
romantic evening, a perfect gift or to create just the right ambience in
your home. A decorative candle can add the missing element that will
transform a setting into something unique.

CANDLELIT
romance

The soft, flattering glow of candlelight is the ideal setting for a romantic dinner, whether it is a first date or a wedding anniversary. Red roses are natural partners for romantic candles, especially old-fashioned roses with heady scents, which are gradually released by the warmth of the flame. Choose large, full-blown roses for maximum romantic impact or tiny rosebuds for a delicate, pretty effect. You can even make the roses part of the candle itself, using hand-pressed petals and leaves collected at the height of summer and saved for a special occasion such as this. Add a few drops of richly perfumed essential oil to the candle or surround it with scented rose potpourri for a deliciously sensuous atmosphere.

On warm summer evenings, the most romantic place to be is outdoors, in the garden or on the patio. Place a dozen or so tiny candles and lanterns round where you are sitting, and some shimmering glass candleholders on a tray scattered with rose petals, jasmine or honeysuckle. As the darkness increases, the tiny stars will compete with the flickering light of the candles. For a lovely romantic holiday, pack a couple of small metal lanterns or shell candles in your luggage and take them with you to the beach in the evening, when seated by the soft, lapping waves of the sea.

ABOVE Light the room entirely with candlelight by arranging a group of different candles together. Here a tin lantern, metal mini-buckets and shell candles give a gentle, warm glow that is magical in the darkness. It is sometimes surprising how so many small candles and nightlights (tea-lights) can create such a vivid, burning, strong light.

RIGHT Scented candles release their perfume in the heat of the flame. Sprinkle a few drops of scented essential oil over the candle before you light it or choose one that is already perfumed. Scented candles will have a dramatic impact on your mood and can therefore be used to help create a new atmosphere in the room.

ABOVE Choose different beautiful candles for different times of the year. Pressed flower candles are lovely in summer, while a spicy gilded candle pot creates a sumptuous mood on long winter evenings. Beeswax candles smell sweetly of warm honey.

LEFT A beautiful rose and a single floating candle in a lovely ornamental leaf-shaped dish are sure to set a romantic mood. This spectacular pink-and-white striped rose is called "Henri Matisse". Allow yourself to come under the spell of a sweet scent, the glitter of water and the warm glow of a burning candle.

scents

An extra dimension is offered by scented candles, which are now immensely popular. They can create a romantic or festive atmosphere; they can also soothe and relax us or lift our spirits, depending which essential oils are used. Lavender oil will induce sleep and help you to unwind, while bergamot or rosemary will revive you. Complement the scent of the candle with a delicate candle collar of lavender or rosemary, to make an attractive decoration or gift. Burning a scented candle while you relax in the bath is wonderfully self-indulgent and your own form of aromatherapy.

Oil lamps are an original alternative to candles, and you can colour and perfume the oil to suit your mood or the occasion. Another variation is to place your chosen essential fragrance, diluted with water, over a candlelit ceramic burner or vaporizer, which will gently warm the oil and release the fragrance. Scented potpourri can be used in the same way and many different kinds are now available, including citrus scents. During Christmas, rich, spicy scents are popular, and you can add extra spice oils to a candle decorated with sticks of cinnamon or studded with cloves. Sprinkle a few drops of oil on the candle before it is lit, being careful not to let the oil fall on any ribbon or fabric in the display. A vaporizer will create an immediate spicy, festive atmosphere if you use it to warm a mixture of succulent orange and cinnamon smelling oils.

ABOVE The spicy scent of cloves makes a richly aromatic winter decoration. The cloves are pressed into the honeycomb sections of a beeswax candle in an attractive spiral pattern. More cloves and rings of star anise cover the base. The result will be a pungent collection of warm aromas.

ABOVE Spices are an important ingredient of many scents, often underlying the sweet floral tones. Experiment with different blends of ingredients, all of which are brought out by the heat of the candle flame.

ABOVE RIGHT This elegant burner houses a large candle instead of a nightlight (tea-light). Lavender is one of the most popular essential oils used in aromatherapy, and it is particularly popular in the evening to soothe and induce rest and sleep.

RIGHT Essential oils can be added to the oil in oil lamps before they are lit. These attractive alternatives to candles are becoming increasingly popular because of their simple elegance and transparency, and they are now available in many different ornamental shapes.

LEFT A ceramic burner, as used in aromatherapy, is a excellent way to perfume a room. Light the nightlight (tea-light) in the bottom chamber then mix your chosen essential oil with water in the bowl on top. The scented oil will vaporize into the air. Choose scents that are personally pleasing or as a means of helping you change your mood after a long, stressful day at work.

FLOATING lights

The combination of light and water is endlessly fascinating and soothing. A water feature is difficult to achieve if you do not have a suitable garden, but you can very simply and instantly add a water display to your home with floating candles, and these lovely little candles are equally practical indoors as well as outside.

Simple round floating candles, either plain or coloured, look very stylish in a plain glass bowl – group a few together so that they bob around the bowl, creating ever-changing patterns of light in the water. Alternatively, you can feature just a single floating candle to show off a beautifully decorated piece of glass, which you may otherwise never use. Floating candles are often moulded into pretty flower shapes,

ABOVE This delicate cone-shaped glass bowl sitting in a black metal frame is specially made to hold a single floating candle. It is very effective if you match the colours of the flowers to the colour of the candle flower.

RIGHT A large hanging glass lantern is an enchanting way to light a dinner table. Place seashells in the bottom, then cover the surface of the water with a cluster of flower candles to resemble an exotic lily pond.

which make an enchanting display if you scatter a few real petals in the water. For a buffet party, use a large bowl of water and float whole flower heads among the candles – bright red and orange gerberas or large white daisies would look fantastic, and the effect is surprisingly simple to achieve.

Fish-shaped floating candles are popular with children, and tiny stars and suns create a magical effect in the evening when the candlelit glass bowl really becomes a focus of attention. This is a very safe way to use candles, so if you are busy entertaining you do not need to keep an eye on them; when the candles burn down you can simply replace them. For extra sparkle, candle shops sell pebble-sized nuggets of coloured glass, which you place in the bottom of the bowl before adding the water. Quite different effects can be created depending on whether you use simply a pale glass colour or deep sea-blues and greens.

ABOVE Floating fish candles swim over a bed of seashells in a beautiful ceramic bowl. Surround the bowl with other seaside bits and pieces to continue the marine theme. This evocative display would be ideal in a bathroom setting or perhaps on a side table in a garden patio.

LEFT Nothing could be simpler or more beautiful than a group of cream candles gently balancing in a simple glass bowl full of water. The shape of the bowl perfectly echoes the rounded shape of the bobbing candles and doesn't detract from the delicate and subtle reflections that are thrown on to the surrounding surfaces.

THE perfect gift

Candles are always very welcome gifts, as not only do they symbolize light and cheerfulness but they also make attractive decorations for the home. For the simplest gift of all, and one that is suitable for all occasions, tie a couple of beautiful church (ivory pillar) candles or beeswax candles with an ornate coloured ribbon. If you are delivering the candles the same day, you could thread the stem of a single rose or lily under the ribbon. Candle pots are popular gifts, especially if you have decorated the collar around the top of the pot yourself. Dried flowers would be appropriate for a birthday, or herbs for someone who is an enthusiastic cook. In either case, finish the candle pot with a ribbon bow in one of the colours in the flowers or herbs, or a simple raffia bow for a country look. The advantage of being able to choose your own design and colours is that you can match them to the tastes of the person concerned.

Christmas is the time for candles as well as for presents. Candle pots and boxes can be decorated with bunches of twigs, dried mushrooms, nuts and whole spices, and you can make several presents at once using the same materials. Festive candles can be stencilled in delicate gold or silver patterns, or for a really special gift you can use pure gold leaf. A lovely idea at Christmas is to make or buy an Advent candle, or candles, which are specially designed to last for the whole month of December.

BELOW Gifts that you have decorated yourself are especially welcome. This candle pot with gold-sprayed pine cones and nuts would make an ideal Christmas gift, and the pansy-decorated candle is a lovely reminder of summertime.

ABOVE Prepare a gift basket full of a collection of simply good things, including a pineapple, a pot plant and two large beeswax candles. These are the best quality of all candles as not only do they burn very slowly but they also scent the room with a delicious smell of honey. Simple bows made from string will make the display special too.

LEFT For a simple, elegant gift, tie a piece of antique gold braid ribbon around a bundle of matching cream church (ivory pillar) candles. This is also a lovely way to display cream or white candles on a mantelpiece until they are ready for use.

MAKING
:::: candles

Nothing beats the satisfaction of making your own hand-made and decorated candles, and it is not at all difficult. You can dye your candles exactly the colours you want to match your furnishings or table setting, and perfume them with your favourite scented oils.

Introduction

Candle-making covers a wide range of techniques, both ancient and modern. The most basic and traditional way to make candles is the dipping method, which has been used for centuries, and the lovely tapered shape of dipped candles is still very popular today. Beeswax also has a long history, and sheets of pure beeswax, smelling of honey, are very simple to roll around a wick. The wax in rolled candles only needs to be gently warmed until it is pliable; it does not need to be heated and melted as in many other techniques.

In the early 19th century, a substance called stearin was developed and found to be an excellent shrinking agent for wax. This revolutionized candle-making because it was now possible to mould the wax into different shapes, including straight-sided candles. Ready-made moulds are available from candle-maker's suppliers in a fantastic range of shapes, including very realistic fruits and cartoon characters.

These moulds can be used again and again or, alternatively, you can make your own moulds from corrugated cardboard or sand. In the first technique, the ridges in the cardboard are embossed on the candle, creating an attractive modern effect. Sand candles are another very simple kind of candle to make, and different grades of sand will give different colours and textures. Shells collected at the beach also make excellent containers for candle wax.

If candles, such as shell candles, don't have a flat base, they may need to be supported so that they will be level and safe when they are

lit. The best and simplest way to do this is by placing them in a shallow decorative bowl with some sand around them. Candles that do have flat bases may still need to have them levelled. Do this by standing them briefly in a saucepan of hot water.

If you are making your own candles, it is very simple to add scent, and you can match the scented oil to the colour of the candle. For example, use citrus scents for yellow and orange candles or lavender oil for blue or mauve candles.

Once you have made your candles, you may want to decorate them. Folk art is a wonderful inspiration for candles with a country feel and you do not need artistic skills to carve, paint or stencil stylized patterns and motifs. For really special occasions, there is nothing to compare with the shimmering delicacy of gold leaf or the rather less expensive gold foil. One of the simplest and most beautiful decorations is with flowers or leaves. These may either be embedded in a thin layer of wax or used as a free-standing collar.

ABOVE Make scented candles and use them to create an atmosphere to match your mood – romantic, relaxing or invigorating.

ABOVE As the wick burns, the flame glows through the wax of stained-glass candles.

materials

The most important ingredient in candle-making is the wax, and there are several different kinds available. The amount of wax you will need for each project depends on the size of the candle you want. If you are using a mould or container of any kind, fill it with water and measure it in a measuring jug (cup) – for every 100 ml (3½ fl oz) of water you will need 90 g (3½ oz) of cold wax. If you melt too much wax, leave it to set and then re-use it another time.

1 BEESWAX SHEETS
Beeswax sheets are available in natural shades of brown or yellow and can be used without any heat (other than warming them with a hairdryer if it is cold) to make simple rolled candles.

2 PARAFFIN WAX
This is the basic wax used in candle-making. It is a colourless, odourless by-product of oil refining and is usually sold in bead or pellet form. It melts at a temperature between 40–71°C (104–160°F). Stearin (see below) is added for moulded candles, but paraffin wax is available with added stearin.

3 BEESWAX PELLETS
This is a completely natural product with a delicious honey smell, available in pellets and sheets. It is expensive and is normally used in combination with other waxes to increase the burning time of a candle. If more than 10 per cent of beeswax is used for a moulded candle, a releasing agent has to be applied to the mould first as the wax will be sticky. It is usually considered too expensive for dipped candles, but if you do use it, you do not need a releasing agent.

4 STEARIN
This is added to paraffin wax to increase its shrinking qualities, so that when it is set the wax can be more easily removed from a mould. Stearin also helps to prevent candles from dripping. It is added to the wax in the proportion 1 part stearin:10 parts wax. If you add too much stearin, it will give the candle a soap-like finish. Always melt the stearin first, then add the dye if making coloured candles and then paraffin wax.

BELOW Uncoloured paraffin wax moulded candles have an elegant simplicity.

5 WICKS
These are usually made from braided strands of cotton and come in different thicknesses to suit the size of the candle, ranging from 1–10 cm (½–4 in). These sizes refer to the diameter of the candle, so you would need a 2.5 cm (1 in) wick for a 2.5 cm (1 in) diameter candle. It is important to use the right wick as if it is too small the flame will be small and may be extinguished. There are special wicks for floating candles.

6 PRIMED WICK
With the exception of dipped candles, wicks need to be primed before you make a candle. Melt a little paraffin wax in a double boiler, immerse the wicks and leave to soak for 5 minutes. Remove the coated wicks, lay them out straight on a baking tray (cookie sheet) lined with greaseproof (wax) paper and leave to harden.

7 WICK SUSTAINERS
These small metal discs, also called wick supports, are used to anchor a wick in candles made in containers. Push the wick into the sustainer, which sits flat on the base of the container.

8 WAX DYE
This is available in disc or powder form. The colour of the molten wax may not be the same as when it sets; some dyes are closer to the end colour than others. It is hard to judge sometimes so if you want to check the colour, place a drop of the molten wax on greaseproof (wax) paper and leave it to set. Most manufacturers provide guidelines as to how much wax a specified amount of dye will colour satisfactorily.

9 MOULD SEAL

This is a putty-like substance, used to make moulds watertight. It may also be used to secure the wick in a mould. It is easy to apply and remove and can be re-used over and over again. Make sure that all traces of mould seal are removed from the wick, as even a small residue will stop it from burning.

10 WAX PERFUMES

These are specially made to be added to candle wax and are usually in liquid form. You can also use essential oils or aromatherapy oils, but not all of them smell attractive when burned, so test them first. Add a few drops of a single perfume or oil to the molten wax, but be careful not to add too much.

11 WAX GLUE

Available in block form, this soft, sticky wax is used to glue pieces of wax together for an appliqué effect and to stick decorations, such as foil, leaves or dried flowers, on to a candle. Melt a small amount in the top of a double boiler and apply it carefully with a fine artist's paintbrush.

equipment

Most candles are made by melting wax at very high temperatures, so it is important both for safety and for success to use the correct equipment and to follow the instructions carefully. Never leave wax melting over heat unattended and make sure that you check the temperature regularly.

1 DOUBLE BOILER

This is essential in candle-making as it prevents the molten wax from overheating and igniting. Ideally, it should be made of stainless steel or aluminium (it can be enamel-coated). To use, boil water in the bottom pan and melt the wax in the top part. Check that the bottom pan doesn't boil dry and top it up with more boiling water as needed. To clean the double boiler after you have poured out the molten wax, wipe around the inside with a dry kitchen towel (dish cloth).

2 WAX THERMOMETER

This special thermometer has a range of 38–108°C (100–225°F). It is very important to check the temperature of molten wax accurately, as it needs to be heated to exact temperatures. Always be extremely careful when melting wax as it can catch alight (on fire) and be as volatile as hot cooking oil.

3 DIPPING CAN

This tall, cylindrical can is used to hold liquid wax when making dipped candles. It can hold a surprisingly large amount of wax. Stand the can in a saucepan of gently simmering water, with the water level as high up the sides of the can as possible. As the water in the pan evaporates, add more boiling water.

4 MOULD AND MOULD BASE

Moulds can be made of plastic, glass, rubber or metal and come in a wide variety of shapes and sizes. Spherical and egg-shaped moulds, made out of metal or plastic and which come apart in the middle, are also available. The more elaborate and ornate moulds are usually made of rubber. Wash and dry all moulds carefully after use. Plastic and rubber moulds will not last as long as metal ones, but are usually less expensive. Glass moulds, unless accidentally broken, last indefinitely.

BELOW A collection of coloured candles is an attractive decoration, even when they are not lit. However, be careful to store them away from direct sunlight.

5 WICKING NEEDLES

Made of steel, these needles are available in various sizes between 10–25 cm (4–10 in). They are used to insert wicks in sand and shell candles, for example, and also to support wicks at the base or top of a mould before you start melting the wax.

6 SPOONS

Use an old wooden spoon to mix the wax dye into the stearin. You do not need to stir the wax while it is melting, but you should stir in the dye thoroughly to make sure the colour is evenly dispersed. Use an old metal spoon for crushing dye discs, but do not stir hot wax with it as this could be dangerous since the spoon will be hot.

7 BAKING TRAY (COOKIE SHEET) AND CAKE TINS (PANS)

An old baking tray (cookie sheet) and cake and roasting tins (pans), lined with greaseproof (wax) paper, are very useful when you are making sheets of wax. A baking tray can also be used as a base for candle moulds. If you use interestingly shaped baking tins, such as petits fours or brioche moulds, as candle moulds, make sure that they have a smooth, rust-free surface and that any leaks are sealed. A roasting tin also makes an excellent water bath for cooling small floating candles while they are setting.

8 GREASEPROOF (WAX) PAPER

This is used to line baking trays (cookie sheets) or pans when you are making sheets of wax. If you have some wax left over from a project, pour it into a lined baking tin (pan) and leave to it set, for use at a later date.

9 CRAFT KNIFE

A craft knife or scalpel with a sharp blade is needed for a variety of purposes. Apart from cutting wicks to length, you can use it to cut sheets of beeswax. When making a stencil or template, you usually get a neater and more accurate edge if you use a craft knife rather than scissors. Always work with a sharp blade, as blunt ones tend to slip, which can cause injury as well as spoiling the work in hand.

CANDLE-MAKING

techniques

■ ■ ■ ■

Depending on what shape you want, candles can be rolled, dipped or moulded, and each of these simple techniques can be adapted to produce more ambitious designs. Experiment with twisted or marbled candles, sand candles, shell candles and hand-moulded wax flowers.

ROLLED beeswax

Beautiful golden candles rolled from thin sheets of natural beeswax are the simplest candles to make. Beeswax comes in pre-formed honeycomb sheets, which are easy to work with. To make them pliable, they need to be at room temperature before you start rolling.

YOU WILL NEED
- wick
- rectangular sheet of beeswax
- scissors or craft knife
- artist's paintbrush
- small quantity of melted beeswax
- container for melted wax

1 Lay the wick across the width of the beeswax sheet and cut it to length with scissors or a craft knife.

2 Make sure the wax is at room temperature. If it is cold and, therefore, brittle, use a hairdryer set at a low temperature to make it pliable without melting it. Gently fold the wax over the wick, with one end protruding slightly. Roll into a cylinder, gently pressing the edge to seal.

3 Prime the protruding end of the wick, so that it is ready for burning, by brushing it gently with a small quantity of melted beeswax.

BELOW You can vary the size and shape of these simple candles. To make a rolled pillar candle, for example, continually build up layers to the required width, joining extra sheets of beeswax by butting the edges closely together. Alternatively, to make a tapering candle, cut off a narrow triangular segment from one long side of the sheet of beeswax. Place the wick on the longer of the short sides and roll up. If you cut diagonally across a rectangular sheet of beeswax, it will allow you to make a pair of tapered candles.

MOULDED shapes

Using ready-made moulds offers an enormous range of possibilities to the amateur candle-maker and calls for only the most basic skills to achieve professional results. Moulds come in all shapes and sizes, from simple geometric shapes to ornate fruit, vegetables and flowers.

YOU WILL NEED

- moulds
- primed wicks (see Materials)
- wicking needles
- mould seal
- measuring jug (cup)
- scales (scale)
- paraffin wax
- stearin (10% of quantity of wax)
- wax dye
- kitchen knife
- double boiler
- wooden spoon
- wax thermometer
- ladle
- scissors

1 Prepare each mould by threading a primed wick, longer than the depth of the mould, through the hole in the base. Tie it securely around the centre of a wicking needle long enough to hold it taut and vertical when the needle is resting across the top of the mould.

2 Pull the other end of the wick taut and press a large blob of mould seal around it to prevent any wax leaking through.

3 Measure out the wax and stearin. Cut some wax dye from a dye disc. Melt the stearin in a double boiler. Add the dye and stir until melted. Add the wax and melt. Using a wax thermometer, turn off the heat when it reaches 93°C (200°F).

MEASURING WAX FOR A MOULD
Fill a mould with water: for 100 ml (3½ fl oz) water, use 90 g (3½ oz) cold wax.

4 Immediately ladle the wax into the mould, taking care not to splash the sides. Tap the mould to release any trapped air bubbles.

5 As the wax starts to set, a slight dip will form around the wick. Prick the surface of the wax all over with a wicking needle.

6 Re-heat the remaining wax to 93°C (200°F) and use to fill up the mould. Let the wax cool completely, then remove the mould seal. The candle should slide out easily. Trim the wick.

EMBOSSED
texture

Corrugated cardboard is an inexpensive way to make simple moulds and gives very stylish results, with the ridged surface of the cardboard embossed on the candle. Spraying the corrugated cardboard before you pour in the wax helps to prevent the wax from sticking to it as it sets.

YOU WILL NEED

- clean plastic container lid
- bradawl (awl)
- corrugated cardboard
- scissors
- water or silicone oil spray
- double-sided tape
- mould seal
- primed wick (see Materials)
- wicking needle
- measuring jug (cup)
- scales (scale)
- paraffin wax
- stearin (10% of quantity of wax)
- double boiler
- wax dye
- wooden spoon
- wax thermometer

1 To make the base of the mould, pierce the middle of the plastic lid with a bradawl (awl) to make a hole big enough to take the wick. Cut a rectangle of corrugated cardboard to size with the width matching the candle height.

2 Spray the cardboard with water or silicone oil to moisten it. Roll it into a cylinder and join the sides with double-sided tape.

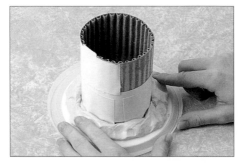

3 Place the cardboard cylinder centrally over the plastic lid. Seal the join with mould seal – the mould must be absolutely watertight.

4 Cut a length of primed wick. Attach one end to a wicking needle, pushing the other end through the hole in the base of the mould. Let the needle rest on top of the cardboard cylinder. Seal the hole in the base with mould seal.

LEFT A selection of light and heavyweight corrugated cardboard can be used to create a group of candles with different size ridges. The natural colours of the candles and cardboard look very contemporary, and packed into a complementary box, they would make a delightful present.

5 Measure the required quantities of paraffin wax and stearin. Melt the stearin in the top of a double boiler. Add the dye until it is the right colour, stirring until thoroughly blended. Add the paraffin wax and heat until it has melted and reaches 82°C (180°F). Pour the wax into the mould, almost to the rim.

6 Leave the candle to cool. Top up around the wick with more molten wax when a well forms as the wax shrinks. When the candle is completely set, peel off the tape and mould seal and remove the cardboard. Trim any excess wick.

MARBLED
spiral

In this very unusual candle the wax is dyed in two contrasting colours, which are kneaded together to mimic the effect of marble. Instead of the rich colours shown here, you could dye the wax paler colours, such as sandy yellow and cream to imitate the natural colours of stone.

YOU WILL NEED

- sharp knife
- 270 g (9½ oz) dip-and-carve wax
- double boiler
- wax dyes in 2 colours
- wooden spoon
- 2 old roasting tins (pans)
- 4 large sheets greaseproof (wax) paper
- rolling pin
- primed wick (see Materials)

1 Cut half the wax into chunks and melt in the top of the double boiler. Stir in the dye. Line a roasting tin (pan) with greaseproof (wax) paper so that it overlaps the sides and pour in the wax. Melt the remaining wax and dye it a contrasting colour and repeat as above.

MAKING THE PAPER TEMPLATE
Draw a 28 x 15 cm (11 x 6 in) rectangle. Mark two points 2 cm (¾ in) in from each corner on one short side. Draw a freehand curved line from each point to the corner at the far end, then cut along the lines.

2 Leave the wax to set slightly, so that it is no longer runny, but it is still pliable. Keep it in a warm atmosphere. Roll both colours of wax into sausage shapes between the greaseproof (wax) paper, then knead the two together, but not so thoroughly that they blend into a single colour.

3 Keeping the wax warm and pliable, put it on a clean sheet of greaseproof (wax) paper on a smooth, flat surface and cover with another sheet. (If it has started to harden, place it in a saucepan on top of a warm oven, but don't let it get so hot that it begins to melt, then place between the sheets of paper.) Use a rolling pin to roll out the wax until it is about 5 mm (¼ in) thick.

4 Remove the top piece of greaseproof (wax) paper. Place the paper template directly on the wax and quickly cut round the edge with a sharp knife, adjusting the size if necessary.

5 Press a length of primed wick along the longer of the short sides of the wax so that about 2 cm (¾ in) protrudes above the top edge. Roll the wax tightly and carefully around the wick, working away from you.

6 Continue to roll up the wax, keeping it as straight as possible. When you get to the end, press the edge into the candle. Trim the base and the wick with a sharp knife. Leave the candle to set for at least 1 hour before burning.

S C E N T E D
candle

Some scented oils are especially produced for candle-making and are available from candle-makers' suppliers. Aromatherapy oils are believed to be therapeutic – choose citrus oils for their uplifting effect, and ylang-ylang or rose oil to relieve anxiety and tension.

YOU WILL NEED

- craft knife
- thin posterboard (card stock)
- small bowl
- rubber mould
- pencil
- scissors
- primed wick (see Materials)
- mould seal
- wicking needle
- measuring jug (cup)
- scales (scale)
- paraffin wax
- double boiler
- wax dye
- wooden spoon
- wax thermometer
- wax perfume or scented oil
- needle

2 Thread a primed wick through the mould. Make the end where the wick will burn watertight by blocking it up with plenty of mould seal. Pull the wick taut, then tie the opposite end firmly around the centre of a wicking needle long enough to rest comfortably across the top of the mould.

4 Pour the wax into the prepared mould, taking care not to touch the sides, as far as the rim. Fill the bowl with cold water and leave the candle to cool for 1 hour. When a dip in the wax forms around the neck, prick the surface with a needle, then add more hot wax. Leave to cool for another hour.

1 Cut a piece of posterboard (card stock) to rest on top of the bowl. Place the mould on the posterboard and draw around it, then cut out. Push the mould into the hole so that the rim at its base is lying flat against the posterboard.

3 Measure the paraffin wax according to the mould. Add the to the top of the double boiler and melt. Add the dye, stirring thoroughly to mix. Keep testing the temperature of the liquid wax. Heat the wax until it reaches 75°C (167°F). Turn off the heat and add a few drops of the wax perfume or oil, stirring.

5 When the wax is completely set and cold, remove the wicking needle and posterboard, then gently peel back the rubber mould. Trim the wick at the base with a craft knife. If necessary, neaten the bottom of the candle by standing it in a warm saucepan for a short amount of time.

roses

These small candles make an enchanting centrepiece for a formal dinner table, surrounded by an arrangement of fresh roses. They would be very romantic for Valentine's Day or a wedding anniversary. Float them in a shallow glass bowl so that the candlelight reflects in the water.

YOU WILL NEED

- scales (scale)
- stearin (10% of quantity of wax)
- double boiler
- red wax dye
- kitchen knife
- wooden spoon
- paraffin wax (quantity according to need)
- wax thermometer
- baking tray (cookie sheet)
- greaseproof (wax) paper
- ladle
- wooden board
- primed wick (see Materials)

1 Measure out and melt the stearin in a double boiler and add the wax dye, as required. Stir until melted and the dye is even. Add the paraffin wax and heat until the mixture reaches 82°C (180°F).

2 Line a baking tray (cookie sheet) with greaseproof (wax) paper and ladle the wax mixture into it in an even layer. When the wax is still warm, peel away the greaseproof paper and place the wax on a wooden board.

3 Using a kitchen knife, roughly cut petal shapes out of the wax.

4 Roll the first petal shape around a piece of primed wick, leaving 2 cm (¾ in) of the wick protruding at the top.

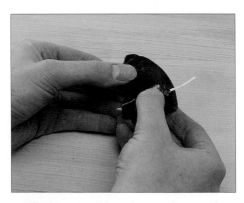

5 Working quickly, take another petal and wrap it around the first, overlapping the edges.

6 Continue to build up layers of petals, adding five or six more petals to create a finished rose. If the wax hardens and becomes too brittle to mould without cracking, re-melt it and start again. Repeat until you have the required number of roses.

BELOW You can make other kinds of flowers in a similar way and in a range of colours. Mix the floating candles with real flowers for a truly stunning display.

shells

The beautiful shapes of large shells make wonderfully decorative natural containers for candle wax. Here a gorgeous group of shell candles in different shapes and sizes nestles in a shallow bowl of sand to support them since the bases of the shells are not flat.

YOU WILL NEED

- selection of shells
- mould seal
- measuring jug (cup)
- scales (scale)
- paraffin wax
- stearin (10% of quantity of wax)
- kitchen knife
- wax dye
- scissors
- primed wick (see Materials)
- wick sustainers
- double boiler
- wooden spoon
- wax thermometer
- ladle
- wicking needle
- lustre paint in gold and silver
- plate for mixing paints

1 Place the shells on a flat surface, sticking them down with small blobs of mould seal if necessary to stop them from wobbling. Using mould seal, block up any holes or cracks to prevent the wax from leaking out of them when it is a hot liquid.

2 To calculate the amount of paraffin wax you will need, fill the shells with some water and measure out the quantity. Weigh out the wax and the required amount of stearin. Cut enough wax dye from a disc to give the depth of colour you want and carefully crush it up using a knife.

3 Cut a length of wick for each shell. A large shell can have the wick supported in the centre with a wick sustainer before the wax is added. It is easier to add a primed wick to smaller shells once the wax has been added.

4 Melt the stearin in a double boiler. Add the dye, stirring until completely melted. Add the wax and melt.

5 The molten wax is ready when it reaches a temperature of 93°C (200°F).

6 Using a ladle, carefully pour the molten wax into the large prepared shell and the small shells.

7 For the small shells, leave the wax until it is set just enough to hold the wicks in place. Position short lengths of primed wick in the centre of each wax-filled shell, making a hole with a wicking needle. Leave a short piece of wick extending above the wax. As the wax shrinks, fill up with more molten wax and leave to cool.

8 Squeeze small amounts of gold and silver lustre paint on to a plate and, using your finger, lightly rub the paint randomly all over the top surfaces of the candles to create a decorative sheen to match the natural pearly interior of the shells.

GLOWING sand candles

This technique is very easy and fun to do. Slightly damp sand makes an excellent candle mould. Bold primary colours contrast well with the natural colour and texture of the sand. For a more ornate finish, the coating can be carved with a surface-forming tool or rasp.

YOU WILL NEED

- damp sand
- large mixing bowl
- small ovenproof bowl
- tape measure
- scissors
- primed wick (see Materials)
- scales (scale)
- stearin (10% of quantity of wax)
- saucepan
- wax dye
- wooden spoon
- paraffin wax
- wax thermometer
- metal spoon
- wicking needle

1 Pour damp sand into the large bowl so that it is half full. Press it down firmly with your fist. Push the smaller bowl into the sand. Some of the sand will be displaced to rise up the sides. Add more sand around the edges, pressing it in very firmly.

2 Carefully remove the small bowl. Measure the depth of the hole. Cut the wick to this length plus 2.5 cm (1 in).

3 Measure the wax needed. Measure and heat the stearin in the saucepan and add the dye. When it is well mixed, add the wax. Take extra care to watch the wax all the time as it is dangerous when hot, and heat it to 127°C (261°F). Remove it from the heat.

4 Gently pour a little wax into the centre of the mould, trickling it over the back of a metal spoon.

LEFT Instead of a plain round bowl, you can use unusual shaped moulds, such as stars.

5 Within 5 minutes the wax will seep into the sand, so fill it with more wax heated to 127°C (261°F). After about 2 hours, a well will form in the middle of the wax. Fill this with more heated wax.

6 Push a wicking needle through the centre of the well, then lower the wick into the hole. Wind the top of the wick around the needle and rest the needle across the sand. Leave the wax to cool for another 3 hours, then lift the candle out of the sand. Trim the wick. Carefully smooth the base of the candle in a warm saucepan or using a medium-hot iron to make sure that it does not wobble.

MOSAIC
candle pots

Cheap glass tumblers are ideal for decorating, as the thick glass is not too delicate to work with. A mix-and-match collection found in junk shops (at flea markets) will look as good as a matching set. Touches of gold on the rims and rubbed on the candle complete the medieval effect.

YOU WILL NEED

- glass tumblers
- craft knife and cutting mat
- small pieces of foam rubber
- ceramic paints in several colours
- plate, for mixing paints
- fine artist's paintbrush
- gold ceramic paint
- measuring jug (cup)
- scales (scale)
- paraffin wax
- stearin (10% of quantity of wax)
- wax dye
- kitchen knife
- primed wick (see Materials)
- scissors
- wicking needles
- double boiler
- wooden spoon
- wax thermometer
- ladle
- gold lustre paint

1 Clean the tumblers thoroughly and leave to dry completely. Using a craft knife and cutting mat, carefully cut the foam rubber into small squares all the same size.

2 Pour a small quantity of ceramic paint in each colour on to a plate. Carefully holding a sponge square, dip it into the paint. Starting at the base of the first tumbler, firmly apply the painted surface to the glass. Alternate the colours until the tumbler is completely decorated. Continue with the other tumblers. Leave to dry thoroughly.

3 Using a fine paintbrush and a little gold ceramic paint, decorate the rim of each tumbler. Leave to dry.

4 Calculate the amount of paraffin wax needed by filling the tumblers with water and measuring it out. Weigh out the correct amount of wax and stearin, and, using a knife, cut off enough wax dye from a disc to give the depth of colour required.

5 For each tumbler, tie a length of primed wick around a wicking needle. Pull it taut and place so it hangs in the centre and just reaches the bottom.

6 Melt the stearin in a double boiler. Add the dye, stirring until completely melted. Add the wax. Keep testing the temperature. When it reaches 93°C (200°F), ladle it into the centre of each tumbler, ensuring that the wax does not splash on to the sides. Tap the sides to release any air bubbles. As the wax cools, a slight dip will form around the wick. Prick the surface of the dipped area all over with a wicking needle and fill up with more melted wax.

7 Leave the wax to set. Use a small brush or your finger to cover each candle lightly with gold lustre paint.

CANDLE
decorating
■ ■ ■ ■

For a special occasion or a gift, you can stencil, paint or carve cold wax
using traditional folk motifs and patterns or your own design. The
ultimate luxury is a candle decorated with gold leaf or natural flowers
and leaves. Church (ivory pillar) candles are best for decorating.

dipped candles

These tall, tapered candles always look stylish and have a unique quality that factory-produced candles cannot match. They are made a pair at a time by dipping a length of wick several times into a deep can of melted wax. It is very satisfying to watch the candles build up layer by layer.

YOU WILL NEED

- paraffin wax
- metal dipping can
- large saucepan
- wooden spoon
- wax thermometer
- sharp knife
- wax dye
- lengths of primed wick (see Materials), 60 cm (24 in) for each pair of 25 cm (10 in) candles

1 Pour the paraffin wax into the dipping can and place in a saucepan. Fill the saucepan with water to reach about halfway up the side of the dipping can. Heat the water to melt the wax, stirring the wax occasionally. Test the temperature with a wax thermometer. When it reaches 71°C (160°F), turn down the heat.

2 Cut pieces of wax dye and add to the wax, stirring to mix thoroughly. The dye is usually quite intense, so do not add too much. (If you want to strengthen the colour after you have made one pair of candles, re-heat the remaining melted wax and add more dye.)

3 Check that the temperature of the wax has not dropped – if it has, increase the heat and bring it back to 71°C (160°F). Hold a length of primed wick in the middle and dip the ends into the wax in a smooth movement so that about 5 cm (2 in) on either side of your fingers remains uncovered. Keep in the wax for about 3 seconds.

4 Leave the dipped wicks to cool for about 3 minutes. Hang them by their wick over two nails so they don't touch. Repeat the dipping and cooling processes until the candles are the thickness you require – this may take anything from 15–30 dips.

5 To give the candles a smooth finish, increase the heat. When the temperature of the melted wax reaches 82°C (180°F), dip the candles in it for about 3 seconds and then leave to cool, hung over two nails. Trim the bases flat with a sharp knife. Leave to cool and set completely, hung over two nails, for at least 1 hour before burning.

CORKSCREW **candles**

A variation on dipped candles is to twist them into these beautiful spirals. A newly dipped candle is quite easy to work with as long as you keep it warm. It takes a little practice to perfect the technique, but part of the charm of these candles is their hand-made quality.

YOU WILL NEED

- newly dipped candle, still malleable
- rolling pin

1 Flatten the candle with a rolling pin on a clean, smooth surface until it is about 5 mm (¼ in) thick. Try not to flatten the base of the candle, but if you do, this can be remedied later.

2 Hold the candle near the wick between the thumb and forefinger of one hand and near the base with your other hand. Keeping the top hand steady, gently twist the candle with the other hand. (Some people find this easier if they hold it upside down.) Work quickly while the wax is warm and pliable enough to respond, but do not be too vigorous.

3 When the candle is twisted fairly evenly along its entire length, check that the base will still fit snugly into a candle holder. If necessary, re-shape it with your fingers so that it is round again. Leave the candle to cool and set completely for at least 1 hour before burning.

STARS
and stripes

Hand-painted patterns make ordinary white or cream candles look really special. Simple motifs such as bands, dots and child-like stars have great folk-art appeal, and once you are confident with the technique you can go on to produce more elaborate designs.

YOU WILL NEED

- plain white or cream candles
- damp cloth
- water-based gouache or poster paints
- fine artist's paintbrush
- darning needle

BELOW Gold paint carefully applied to white candles adds a touch of elegance and an almost medieval quality. Even simple patterns can create a variety of effects.

1 Wipe the surface of the candle with a damp cloth and dry it carefully. To make the star design, mark equally spaced dots of paint all over the candle. Take care not to smudge the paint as you work.

2 Make each dot into an asterisk, then thicken the lines to make the asterisk into a star. When the paint is completely dry, scratch a spiral in the centre of each star with a darning needle.

carving

Carved candles have a wonderful three-dimensional quality, achieved by cutting through an outer layer of coloured wax to reveal the white or cream base candle underneath. The carving isn't difficult, but remember that straight, tapered lines are much easier to cut than curves.

YOU WILL NEED
- white egg-shaped candle with dipped coloured outer coating
- small and large V-shaped lino-cutting tools (linoleum knives)
- small decorator's paintbrush

BELOW As long as they have been dipped in a colour coating, any shape of candle can be carved. Choose any pattern or motif you like, but the decoration is most effective when it is simple and symmetrical.

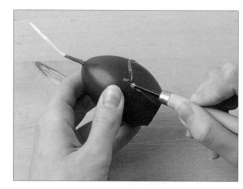

1 Using the small lino-cutting tool (linoleum knife), cut a line from the wick to the base of the candle. Begin with a shallow line, then cut again to reveal the white wax underneath.

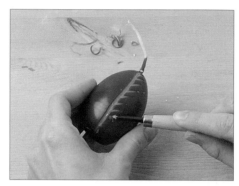

2 Starting at the wick and working down towards the base, cut small lines branching off the original line to create a long, feathery effect. Place the lino-cutting tool the required distance from the long line and work towards it, rather than starting from the line and working outwards.

3 Use a small paintbrush to remove any wax debris carefully as you work. Repeat the feathered line design on the other side of the candle, directly opposite the first, so that the candle's surface is halved.

4 Cut a star-shaped flower in the centre of each half, cutting from the centre to the outer edge. Cut the petals lightly at first and leave a circle of wax uncut in the middle of the flower, if you wish. Then use the larger lino-cutting tool to carefully trace over the pattern again, and define and deepen the petals to emphasize their shape.

5 Brush away the wax debris as before. If necessary, tidy up the carving using the small cutting tool (linoleum knife).

PATTERNED
candles

This is a very effective way to decorate a set of candles for a special occasion, such as a wedding, because once you have drawn your design and cut the stencil you can repeat it as many times as you like. An even simpler method is to use lace or paper shelf edging as a "stencil".

YOU WILL NEED

- church (ivory pillar) candles
- tape measure
- stencil card (card stock)
- pencil
- ruler
- craft knife and cutting mat or scissors
- spray adhesive or masking tape
- gold and silver non-toxic spray paints
- lace or paper shelf edging

1 Measure the height and circumference of the candle. Draw a design on stencil card (card stock) to fit. Cut out the parts of the design to appear on the candle.

2 Coat the back with spray adhesive and stick it to the candle or hold in place with masking tape. Apply the spray paint, let dry and remove the stencil.

3 Another method that does not require you to make a stencil is to cut lengths of lace or paper shelf edging to fit around the candle. Hold the pattern in place with masking tape, then spray on the paint. Leave to dry completely before removing the lace or paper "stencil" so that it does not smudge.

PRESSED flower candles

A lovely way to use pressed summer flowers is to trap them beneath a thin layer of melted wax on the surface of a plain candle. Alternatively, simply attach them to the melted surface of a candle. Any small flowers are suitable, and you can also add individual petals and leaves.

YOU WILL NEED

- deep, narrow saucepan
- short, fat church (ivory pillar) candle
- small pressed flowers
- selection of small, flat silver-coloured decorative shapes
- tweezers

1 Fill the saucepan with boiling water. Holding one end of the candle, dip the other end into the water for about 4–5 seconds. Remove the candle from the water and immediately stick on as many of the pressed flowers and metal decorations as you can before the wax hardens again.

DRYING FLOWERS

The easiest way to dry flowers is to hang them upside-down in small bunches in a warm, well-ventilated, dark place (sunlight causes the colour to fade). Pick flowers for drying after the dew has evaporated and when their colour and bloom are at their best. Handle them carefully, as they become very fragile when dried.

2 Repeat the process, turning the candle each time. Do not leave it in the water for too long in case the wax also melts around the parts of the candle that have already been decorated. Use tweezers, if necessary, to push heavier items, such as rose buds, into the wax, but handle these delicate materials carefully.

J E W E L L E D
candles

This exotic effect is created by decorating richly coloured candles with gold foil from chocolate wrappers, cut into delicate shapes. Applied to the surface of the candle with a heated bodkin, the foil resembles gold leaf. The design is then embellished with sparkling sequins and beads.

YOU WILL NEED

- gold foil from chocolate wrappers
- craft knife and cutting mat
- metal ruler
- pencil
- small, sharp scissors
- coloured spherical or pillar candle
- bodkin
- nightlight (tea-light), for heating bodkin
- matches
- assortment of small beads and sequins
- dressmakers' pins
- strong clear glue
- small flat-backed sparkling decorations

2 Using small, sharp scissors or a craft knife, cut out the star motif, then carefully open out the foil.

4 Place the gold foil strips, one at a time, in position on the candle, forming a criss-cross pattern around the star motifs. Heat the bodkin again in the flame of the nightlight for a few seconds to hold the strips in place. Pick up a small bead on a dressmakers' pin, then a sequin. Heat the pin briefly in the flame of the nightlight and push it into the candle at one of the points where the foil strips cross. Repeat at all the points where the foil strips cross.

1 With your fingers, gently smooth the creases out of the gold foil, taking care not to tear it. Cut out four or more long strips, depending on the size of the candle, each about 3 mm (⅛ in) wide, using a craft knife and cutting mat and a metal ruler. Then cut out two more 4 cm (1½ in) squares from the gold foil, or more if needed. Fold each square into eight and draw a star design in pencil.

3 Place one foil star in position on the candle, then heat a bodkin in the flame of the nightlight (tea-light) for a few seconds until the pointed end is quite warm. Run the side of the pointed end of the warm bodkin over the foil to melt the wax underneath and so fuse the foil star to the candle. Position a second star on the opposite side of the candle, so that it is symmetrical, and seal in position with a bodkin in the same way.

5 Glue a flat-backed, sparkling decoration in the centre of each star.

PURE
gold

These delicate gold designs are traced in gold leaf on to white or cream candles, but they would look equally good on darker colours, such as crimson. Real gold leaf is expensive, so unless you are confident drawing freehand, it is safest to draw your design first on tracing paper.

YOU WILL NEED

- fibre-tip pen
- tracing paper
- gold leaf transfer
- cream or white candles
- masking tape
- scissors
- ballpoint pen or blunt-ended instrument

1 Draw your design in fibre-tip pen on tracing paper – the sheets between the gold leaf transfer are ideal because they match the gold leaf exactly in size.

2 Position a sheet of gold leaf transfer, gold side against the candle, and hold firmly in place with masking tape. Place the traced design over the gold leaf. Hold it lightly in place with masking tape so that you can lift it off and re-position it later. Draw over the design with a ballpoint pen or blunt instrument – embellish your basic design at this stage if you want to.

LEFT Gold leaf is quite difficult to work with, but the effect – even of simple designs – is stunning.

3 Gently and carefully peel back the gold leaf transfer, checking that the entire design has been successfully transferred to the candle. If necessary, replace the gold leaf and trace any faint or missing parts again.

4 Using fresh sheets of gold leaf, and re-using the tracing paper design, repeat the process all over the candle. As more of the surface candle becomes covered with the gold decoration, take care not to stick masking tape on to areas where the gold leaf has already been applied, as the adhesive will lift it off.

DELICATE hearts

Decorate a plain candle with heart motifs and a simple geometric border for a traditional country-style look. The hearts are stamped out of a flat sheet of deep red wax with a biscuit (cookie) cutter. The border design is done with small squares of sponge and aquamarine paint.

YOU WILL NEED

- sponge, about 2 cm (¾ in) thick
- fibre-tip pen
- craft knife
- old baking tray (cookie sheet)
- greaseproof (wax) paper
- paraffin wax
- double boiler
- deep red wax dye
- wooden spoon
- heart-shaped biscuit (cookie) cutter
- plate, for mixing paint
- aquamarine water-based paint
- washing up liquid (dishwashing detergent)
- white or cream candle
- wax glue
- fine artist's paintbrush

BELOW Appliqué motifs can also be designed to run down the length of a taller candle, rather than around the circumference.

1 Using a fibre-tip pen, draw on the sponge four small squares so that together they make one larger square. Cut out half the depth of the sponge on two diagonally opposite squares.

2 Line the baking tray (cookie sheet) with greaseproof (wax) paper. Melt a small quantity of wax in the top of a double boiler and add the dye. Stir until well blended. Pour the molten wax into the lined baking tray. Tilt the tray to spread out the wax evenly. Keeping the wax warm by placing it in the oven so that it remains pliable, use the cutter to stamp out as many hearts as you need to encircle the candle.

3 Mix the paint with a little washing up liquid (dishwashing detergent) to the consistency of double (heavy) cream. Lightly dip the sponge into the paint, then press it on to the top and bottom edges of the candle. Dip the sponge into the paint again as needed, but do not allow it to become too wet. When both borders are complete, leave them to dry.

4 If the wax hearts have hardened, warm them in the oven or on top of a radiator until malleable. Press a heart against the candle so that it curves. Melt a little wax glue, paint one side of the heart with it and press it firmly on the candle. Add more hearts at equal intervals.

BAY LEAF border

This lovely idea is a perfect example of how often the simplest designs are the best. The glossy dark green of the bay leaves contrasts beautifully in colour and texture with the creamy tones of the church (ivory pillar) candles, and the raffia is a perfect finishing touch.

YOU WILL NEED

- strong clear glue
- about 8 fresh bay leaves for each candle
- church (ivory pillar) candles
- green raffia
- scissors

1 Place a small blob of glue on the back of each bay leaf and stick them vertically around the bottom of the candle. Place the leaves so that they are slightly overlapping each other.

2 When the glue is dry, tie the raffia securely around the centre of the bay leaf border.

3 Trim the ends of the raffia. A simple knot suits this design better than a large bow. It is a sensible precaution to extinguish the candle before it burns down to the level of the bay leaves.

BELOW Other leaves – edible or not – can be used in a similar way, but in this case, they almost completely enclose the candle to create the impression of an exotic vegetable.

C R E A T I V E
····candleholders

Beautiful candles deserve beautiful candleholders, and there is an enormous range of designs here to choose from. Many of the projects you can make yourself; others show ingenious or novel ways to transform a plain candlestick or candelabra into something very special.

Introduction

Candleholders can take a huge variety of forms, from a simple wooden candlestick to an elaborate chandelier or a lavish table display. Candlesticks and candelabra can be made of many unusual materials, as well as traditional wood and metal. Clay, papier-mâché and salt dough can all be moulded into candlestick shapes, and decoration can be added with mirrored mosaic or rope. Ordinary wire twisted into decorative shapes makes a highly individual candelabra or an interesting decoration for a plain candlestick.

Candleholders that enclose the flame are safer than free-standing candles, which may be an important consideration depending on where you wish to place your candles. Candle pots are popular – terracotta pots with the candles secured in fireproof plastic foam. Weathered flowerpots create an attractive rustic look. The base of the candle is decorated with a "collar" of dried flowers, pine cones or nuts, so always remember to extinguish the candle before it burns down to this level. Boxes are a variation on the candle-pot theme, using decorative gift boxes or a plain cardboard box covered with leaves.

Lanterns have a magical quality, whether they are traditional Jack o' Lanterns or fragile paper. Pumpkin lanterns are very safe when children are around because they contain small nightlights (tea-lights) with the flame enclosed inside the lantern. Hand-made paper lanterns, however, should never be left unattended when the candles are lit.

An inspiring variety of sconces and chandeliers include some made of driftwood or decorated with natural woodland materials.

ABOVE Lanterns are perfect for lighting the garden, since the candle flame is protected.

BELOW Silver and brass are the most popular, but other metals also make fine candlesticks.

CANDLESTICKS AND

candelabra

■ ■ ■ ■

Modern variations on this traditional theme feature highly original candlesticks made of driftwood, salt dough or rope, or simple ways to decorate a ready-made candlestick. Wonderful candelabra can be constructed from papier-mâché, wire and even a branch of hazel.

candlesticks

New or previously painted candlesticks can be subtly aged and mellowed. An antiquing patina is applied and then the grooves in the candlestick are picked out with bands of paint in two complementary shades. Candlesticks with accentuated grooved shapes are ideal for this.

YOU WILL NEED

- wooden candlestick
- wax candle
- off-white emulsion (latex) paint
- small, flat paintbrush
- fine sandpaper
- antiquing patina
- rag
- fine artist's paintbrush
- acrylic paints in smoke blue and jade green
- matt (flat) varnish
- varnishing brush

BELOW A vast range of different paint finishes can be applied to inexpensive wooden candlesticks for a stunning effect.

1 Rub the candlestick with the candle, applying a light coating of wax to any pointed edges and raised areas, which would be most likely to be damaged through wear and tear.

2 Paint the candlestick with off-white emulsion (latex) paint and leave to dry. If the wood still shows through the paint, apply a second coat of off-white and leave to dry thoroughly.

3 Lightly rub over the painted candlestick, using fine sandpaper, to give a scuffed surface. Take the paint right back to the original wood in a few places but do not overdo it.

FAR RIGHT For the taller, golden candlestick, gold paint was applied and left to dry, followed by a layer of craquelure (crackle) base varnish brushed on evenly so that no drips formed. When this was dry, a layer of craquelure (crackle) varnish was applied. Finally, when dry, antiquing wax was rubbed into the cracks.

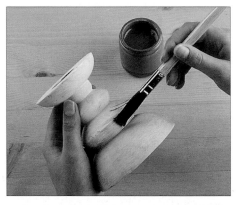

4 Apply a coat of antiquing patina. Lift off some of the patina with a clean rag to mellow the painted surface and provide additional texture.

5 Using a fine artist's paintbrush, roughly paint bands of smoke blue around the top and bottom of the candlestick, and inside any grooves. Don't be too precise – uneven edges will give the best effect. Leave to dry.

6 Roughly paint thin lines of jade green within the smoke blue bands. Leave to dry thoroughly, then brush an even coat of matt (flat) varnish all over the candlestick and leave to dry.

SPIRALLED wire decoration

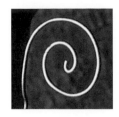

Add an individual touch to a plain candlestick with this simple wire spiral. It would look equally stylish on a natural or painted wooden candlestick, or a frosted glass candlestick as shown here. For an even more decorative look, thread tiny glass beads on to the wire.

YOU WILL NEED

- 1 mm (¹⁄₃₂ in) copper wire
- round-nosed pliers
- wire-cutters
- paper and pencil (optional)
- candlestick

1 Grip the end of the copper wire with a pair of round-nosed pliers and bend a loop. Trim the end with wire-cutters.

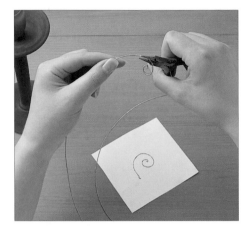

2 Work along the wire, bending it gently to form a spiral. If you wish, you can draw a spiral shape on paper first, so that you have a pattern to follow. This will ensure that if you are decorating a pair of candlesticks, they will match.

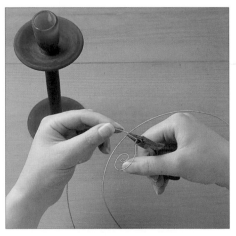

3 Bend the wire to a 45° angle. Grip the wire just below the "elbow" and bend to 90° so that the corner doubles back on itself slightly.

LEFT This more complicated and intricate candle sconce is made from a series of coiled wire spirals.

4 Hold the spiral at the top of the candlestick stem with one hand. With the other, press the loose end of the wire around the stem and tuck it behind the spiral. Then bend the loose end tightly back on itself, so that it locks the wire securely in place.

5 Continue to hold the spiral firmly in position with one hand as you pull the remaining wire tightly down and evenly around the stem of the candlestick with the other. Finally, neatly trim the end of the wire next to the stem with the wire-cutters.

candlestick

This wonderfully original candlestick is created out of weathered wood and seabirds' feathers collected on a beach at low tide. Odd bits of fishing tackle could be added as extra decoration if you wish, but pebbles or shells would probably be too heavy.

YOU WILL NEED

- 2–3 pieces thin driftwood
- glue gun and sticks
- florist's wire
- 2 feathers
- craft knife
- candle

1 Using a glue gun, glue the driftwood pieces together. Leave to dry.

2 Bind a piece of wire around the join (seam). Fashion it into two candelabra-shaped arms.

3 Attach a feather to the end of each candelabra arm by placing a dot of glue on the end of the wire and gently inserting it into the quills.

4 Using a craft knife, make a small hole in the end of a candle to ensure that it will be stable in the candlestick.

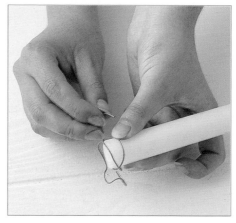

5 Cut a short length of florist's wire, and wind it around the base of the candle.

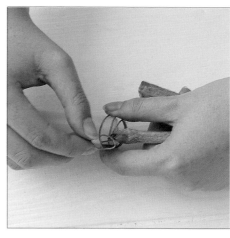

6 Insert a small piece of the driftwood candlestick into the base of the candle. Secure by tightening the wire.

SAFETY HINT

For safety reasons, make sure that the candlestick stands securely on its driftwood legs before use and that the candle is firmly wired into position. Display the candlestick as a sculptural piece – but if you do decide to light the candle, remember to extinguish it before it burns down to the wood.

COILED
pots

This sturdy pair of matching candlesticks is made out of an unusual material, home-made salt dough. The sausage-shaped coils of dough are built up around a chicken-wire frame that supports the structure. When complete, the dough is baked in a low oven until it is hard.

YOU WILL NEED

- wire-cutters
- chicken wire
- ruler
- 1.2 mm galvanized wire
- 0.3 mm galvanized wire
- salt dough (see recipe)
- modelling tool
- baking tray (cookie sheet)
- large artist's paintbrush
- white matt emulsion (latex) paint
- blue acrylic paint
- matt (flat) polyurethane varnish
- varnish brush

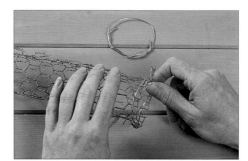

2 Cut two lengths of the thicker galvanized wire. Bend to form rings, one 6 cm (2½ in) in diameter for the base; the other 5 cm (2 in) in diameter for the top. Place the smaller ring over the top of the cylinder. Bend over the ends of the chicken wire to hold it in place.

4 Roll pieces of salt dough into long sausage shapes, about as thick as your index finger.

5 Beginning at the base, wrap the sausage shapes around the cylinder in a spiral, pressing the dough lightly on to the chicken-wire base.

1 Using wire-cutters, cut a 15 x 20 cm (6 x 8 in) rectangle of chicken wire. Bend it along its length to form a cylinder, twisting the ends at the seam.

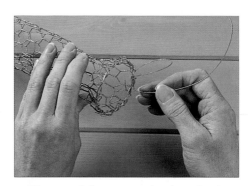

3 "Oversew" the ring with a length of thinner wire. Attach the base ring in the same way. Squeeze the cylinder to make it slightly narrower towards one end.

6 Moisten a modelling tool and gently smooth out the joins (seams) between the coils of dough. Transfer the candlestick to a baking tray (cookie sheet) and bake at 120º/250ºF/Gas ½ for about 10 hours, or until completely dry. Prime the candlestick with a coat of white emulsion (latex), then colour with blue acrylic paint. When dry, apply four coats of matt (flat) polyurethane varnish, allowing each coat to dry before applying the next.

SALT DOUGH RECIPE
Combine 2 cups plain (all-purpose) flour and 1 cup salt in a large mixing bowl, using the same cup measure. Add ½ cup tepid water and mix with a wooden spoon. Add more water until you have a firm dough; if the dough becomes too sticky, add more flour. Dust your hands with flour and knead the dough on a work surface for at least 10 minutes, until elastic. Leave to rest in a plastic bag at room temperature for 30 minutes. Unused dough can be kept in the fridge for up to 3 days.

candleholder

Geometric coils of natural jute rope make a strong, satisfying contrast to the smooth texture of creamy-coloured candles. The construction of the candlesticks is very solid, with an MDF (medium-density fiberboard) base so make sure that you wear protective clothing for this project.

YOU WILL NEED

- pencil
- paper
- scissors
- 1 cm (½ in) sheet of MDF (medium-density fiberboard)
- jigsaw
- protective clothing
- wood saw
- tape measure
- wooden broom handle
- glue gun and glue sticks
- jute rope
- two 7 cm (2¾ in) diameter terracotta plant pot saucers
- small screws
- hammer
- screwdriver

1 Scale up the templates. Draw on the MDF (medium-density fiberboard) and cut out, wearing protective clothing.

2 Saw a 20 cm (8 in) length from the broom handle. Squeeze a little glue on one end. Wind the end of some jute rope into a spiral and press on to it.

3 Squeeze a few lines of glue along the shaft for about 5 cm (2 in) and wind the rope tightly around it. Working in sections, continue until the shaft is completely covered. Finish with a small spiral at the other end of the shaft.

4 Turn the terracotta saucers upside-down. Using a small screw and a hammer, gently tap a hole through the centres. Glue a saucer to the top of each candlestick arm and screw in place.

5 Wrap the arms with rope, using the glue gun. At the edge of a saucer, fray and flatten out the end and glue. Glue and wind on the rope in rows, covering the end. Continue down the arm up to the curve and glue the arm to the candlestick.

6 Glue the rope along both sides of the seam where the arm meets the shaft. To cover the remainder of the arm, glue the rope in concentric rows forming a triangular pattern as shown. Attach the other arm to the shaft of the candlestick and cover both sides of the seam and the remainder of the arm with rope in the same way.

7 Cover the centre with a spiral of rope, working from the outside to the centre.

8 Glue the three legs, evenly spaced, around the base of the candlestick shaft. Cover with rope, beginning at the foot and working up towards the seam. Cover the seam with a concentric triangular pattern as before.

MIRRORED
mosaic stick

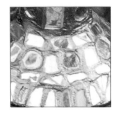

This is a perfect accompaniment to shimmering candlelight, as the faceted surfaces of the mirror pieces reflect the flame. Mosaic mirror tiles have a mesh backing, which helps hold the pieces in place when you break them. Circular mirror pieces are available in ethnic shops.

YOU WILL NEED

- craft knife
- mosaic mirror tiles
- old cloth
- hammer
- powdered tile adhesive
- old table knife
- candlestick
- small round mirror pieces
- medium and fine artist's paintbrushes
- gold acrylic paint

BELOW This attractive mosaic sconce has an appealing North African quality.

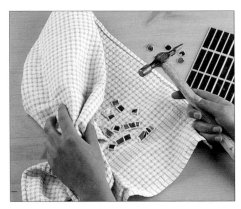

1 Using a craft knife, cut through the backing of a mirror tile, and wrap a segment in a cloth. Break up the mirror into smaller pieces with a hammer. Take care not to cut yourself on any sharp edges. Wear protective gloves if you can work effectively with them on.

2 Following the manufacturer's instructions, mix up the tile adhesive with water to form a fairly thick paste. Apply the adhesive to the candlestick with a table knife, working on a small area at a time. While the paste is still wet, stick on fragments of mirror and the small round mirror pieces. Continue until the whole candlestick is covered.

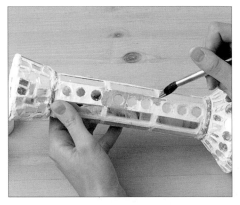

3 When the adhesive is completely dry, use a medium paintbrush to paint the larger areas of white adhesive with gold acrylic, taking care not to cover the pieces of mirror. Load just the tip of the brush with paint and try to keep your hand as steady as possible. If you do get paint on any of the mirror pieces, try removing it immediately with a cotton bud (tip) barely moistened with water.

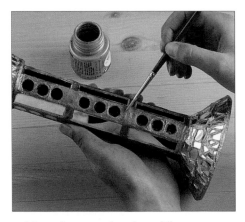

4 Use a fine paintbrush to fill in any gaps around the edges of the pieces of mirror with gold, acrylic paint. Leave the candlestick to dry completely and, if necessary, apply one or even two further coats of paint.

clay holder

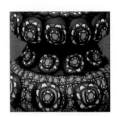

Multi-coloured slices of polymer clay make the intricate, jewel-like patterns used to decorate the surface of this charming little candlestick. The base is simply a suitable wooden object, such as a salt shaker, with a candleholder moulded out of clay positioned on the top.

YOU WILL NEED

- polymer clay in yellow, purple, turquoise, white and black
- rolling pin
- blade
- wooden base that will withstand low heat (120°C/250°F/Gas ½), such as a salt shaker
- sandpaper

BELOW Wooden candleholders painted with autumnal fruit and vine designs create a seasonal theme. The berried branches and yellow candles combine with the soft flames to create a warm but bright display that is reminiscent of a historical pot design.

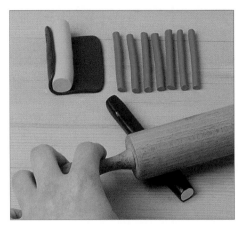

1 Cover a log of yellow clay with a sheet of purple. Roll six thin turquoise logs. Cover a long white log with a sheet of black and square it off by gently rolling it on four sides. Halve diagonally lengthways to make two triangular logs. Slice each length into three widthways to make six triangular logs in total.

2 Place the black-and-white logs and turquoise logs around the purple log. Wrap in a sheet of black to create a "cane". Slice it in half. Set one half aside. Carefully roll the other half on a smooth table surface to reduce the diameter.

3 Keep reducing the cane, slicing it in half, then reducing it again until you have several canes of different diameters. Join tiny canes together. Slice the canes into sections about 3 mm (⅛ in) thick.

4 Lightly sand the base. Mould some black clay into a cup at the top of the base for the candleholder. Cover the middle with a sheet of black. Apply a layer of clay slices, from the bottom up, pressing them on firmly. Bake at 120°C/ 250°F/Gas ½ for 30–45 minutes. Leave to cool, then complete the decoration to form a raised pattern. Bake as before.

TWISTED tree design

A contorted branch of twisted hazel looks like a fantastic tree planted in a gravel mound, and when the candles are lit it is like a scene out of a fairytale. Use a single hazel branch or graft on extra branches to achieve an attractive shape. Remember to position the candleholders carefully.

YOU WILL NEED

- large plastic sheet
- paper towels
- rubber (latex) gloves
- quick-drying clay
- twisted hazel (or similar) branch
- wire cake rack
- tile adhesive grout and spreader
- aquarium gravel
- two-part epoxy putty
- candles
- sharp stick
- non-flammable brown water-based ink
- medium artist's paintbrush
- scissors
- aluminium foil

2 Wearing the gloves, spread the grout over the clay and sprinkle with gravel.

3 Press the gravel firmly into the grout evenly all over the clay.

4 Mix some epoxy putty and roll into balls. Press on to the tips of selected branches. Using your thumb, shape into cups large enough to fit your candles.

1 Protect your work surface with a large plastic sheet and plenty of paper towels. Wearing rubber (latex) gloves to protect your hands, make a large mound out of the clay and firmly embed the hazel branch in it so that it stands firmly. Leave the clay mound to dry, which will take around two days, then carefully place it on a cake rack to allow the bottom to dry out completely.

5 Using a sharp stick, gently scratch vertical lines into the outside of each candleholder, without distorting the shape, to give them a rough, natural-looking texture.

6 Paint the cups with non-flammable brown ink and set the candelabra aside to dry completely. Cut strips of aluminium foil and fold them twice – they must be deep enough to line the candleholders to the rim in order to prevent the edges from burning. Wrap each strip of foil around your thumb and pinch it in at the bottom, then smooth it gently into the candleholder. For safety, extinguish the candles before they burn right down and replace them with new ones the same size.

P A P E R
candelabra

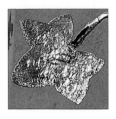

The main ingredients for this wonderful structure are three wire coathangers, some garden wire, torn newspaper and glue. The ivy leaves are cut out of card (card stock) and attached to thin wire stalks, and the main stem twines around the central support very realistically.

YOU WILL NEED
- pliers
- 3 wire coathangers
- jam jar
- pencil
- pair of compasses (compass)
- ruler
- heavy corrugated cardboard
- craft knife
- cutting mat
- thin garden wire
- gummed paper tape
- sponge
- scissors
- thin card (card stock)
- newspaper
- PVA (white) glue
- mixing bowl
- hand-made paper
- masking tape
- papier-mâché pulp (see recipe)
- fine sandpaper
- acrylic varnish
- fine artist's paintbrush
- gold and silver gouache paints

PAPIER-MÂCHÉ PULP

This pulp can be used to make all kinds of candleholder shapes, and it is very easy to work with. Tear up newspaper and boil in water until the paper disintegrates. Squeeze out the excess water, then process in a kitchen blender until reduced to a pulp. Add equal parts of fine sawdust, PVA (white) glue and powdered interior filler, plus a little wallpaper paste (without fungicide). Knead the pulp to a working consistency, adding more water, if too dry, or more interior filler, if too wet. Store in clear film (plastic wrap). Ready-made papier-mâché pulp is also available to mix with water.

1 Using pliers, bend two of the wire coathangers to make two curved arms for the candelabra. Bend the wire around a jam jar to make sure that you create a balanced, smooth shape. Break the hooks off the coathangers.

2 Draw a 15 cm (6 in) diameter circle on the corrugated cardboard and cut it out. Using pliers and a jam jar as before, bend the lower end of each wire arm into a semi-circle to fit around the edge of the cardboard. Bind the two arms securely together with garden wire to make the central support. Attach the cardboard base to the wires with gummed paper tape.

3 To make the candleholders, cut two 9 cm (3½ in) circles of thin card (card stock). Cut a slit to the centre, twist into cone shapes and secure with tape. Tear newspaper strips and soak in PVA (white) glue diluted with water (equal parts). Cover the cones with a layer of papier-mâché. Push them on to the ends of the wire arms and secure with tape.

4 Twist long strips of newspaper and wrap them around the wire frame, securing the twists with garden wire. Soak strips of hand-made paper in diluted PVA glue and cover the structure with a layer of papier-mâché.

5 Bend the third wire coathanger to make the ivy stem. Draw eight to ten ivy leaf shapes on thin card (card stock), cut out and tape each one to a short length of garden wire. Use the wire stalks to attach the leaves to the ivy stem and secure with masking tape. Cover the ivy stem and stalks with strips of hand-made paper.

6 Using garden wire, attach the ivy stem to the main frame, twisting it decoratively around the candelabra. Cover the whole candelabra with papier-mâché pulp. Leave to dry completely in a warm place. Lightly sand the papier-mâché, then spray with varnish. Decorate with gold and silver gouache paints and varnish again.

TWISTED
wire holder

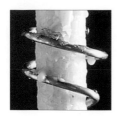

Copper wire is easy to bend and mould into candlesticks or this elegant modern candelabra. You can probably twist the wire stem with your hands, and other shapes such as circles can simply be bent round a can. You can make the design as simple or as ornate as you choose.

YOU WILL NEED

- hacksaw
- heavy-gauge copper wire
- tape measure
- fibre-tip pen
- pliers
- spray paint can or similar
- broom handle or similar

1 Using a hacksaw, cut three pieces of copper wire each 90 cm (36 in) long. Use a fibre-tip pen to mark each piece of wire 30 cm (12 in) and 56 cm (22 in) from one end.

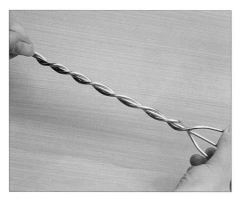

2 Hold the three wires together, with the marked points matching, and, keeping the central wire straight, twist the other two strands around it between the two marked points, keeping it as even as possible. You should be able to do this using your hands, but it may help to use a pair of pliers.

3 At the bottom of the candelabra (with the longer sections of untwisted wires), bend the centre of one piece into a circular shape around a spray paint can or similar object. Using a pair of pliers, continue to bend the end of the wire around inside the circle to make smaller concentric circles until all the wire has been used up. Repeat to make the other two feet of the candelabra.

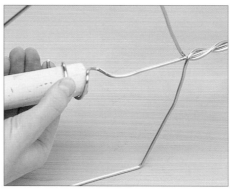

4 At the top of the candelabra, beginning with the central wire, twist the end around a wooden mould, such as a broom handle, the same thickness as the candles you intend to use. Work two or three twists into the wire, then ensure that the rest of the wire above the twisted section is vertically in line.

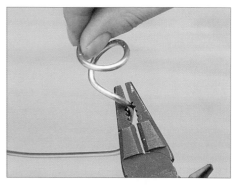

5 To shape the two outer pieces of wire, use pliers to bend them up into a vertical position approximately 10 cm (4 in) from the top of the twisted section of the candelabra.

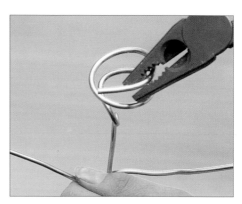

6 Use the broom handle, as before, to twist the ends of the outer wires into circles to form the two outer candleholders. Then neaten all three candleholding sections with pliers.

HELPFUL HINTS
Stand the twisted wire candelabra up and carefully position the three feet on a flat surface to ensure a completely stable base. The copper colour is complemented by beeswax candles.

SAILING boat

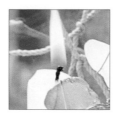

Children will love this delightful little boat and will enjoy searching the beach for treasures to decorate it. The sturdy driftwood structure is joined with pole supports, making it a stable base for candles. The sails are outlined with nuggets of cloudy glass, which shine in the candlelight.

YOU WILL NEED

- hand drill
- 2 pieces flat driftwood
- sturdy stick, for the mast
- 5 pole supports
- screwdriver
- small screws
- hand saw
- glue gun and glue sticks
- pieces of glass and china from the sea
- thick and fine copper wire
- pliers
- 3 small hooks
- shells
- candles and candle stickers

BELOW The beach is a source of interesting materials, but is also a wonderful inspiration.

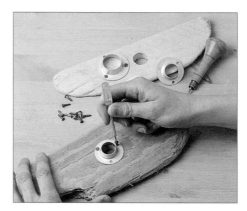

1 Drill a hole the same diameter as the stick that will form the mast through both flat pieces of driftwood. These will form the base and the candle support shelf. Screw a pole support over the hole in each piece of wood.

2 Saw the stick to the required length for the mast. Attach the bottom of the mast firmly to the pole support in the base piece of driftwood, using a small screw and glue, if necessary. Push the mast through the hole in the candle support shelf and attach it firmly in the same way. Screw the other three pole supports on to the top of the shelf to act as candleholders.

3 To make the sails, twist the glass and china between two lengths of thick wire, using a pair of pliers. Bind them in place with fine wire. You will need two sails that are long enough to hang between the top of the mast and the ends of the candle support shelf.

4 Finish the sails with wire loops. Screw a hook into the top of the mast and another at each end of the candle support. Slip a loop from each sail over the hook at the top of the mast, then over the hooks at either end of the support shelf. Decorate the shelf by gluing on shells. Insert the candles, using candle stickers, if necessary.

copper pipe

Burnished copper pipes and coloured marbles reflect the flickering glow from the candles in this stunning candelabra. It takes patience to assemble all the different components, but the result will be the focus of attention. Plumber's suppliers have a wide range of pipes and joints.

YOU WILL NEED
- ruler or tape measure
- pipe cutter
- copper pipe
- 5 copper reducers to fit pipes 19–16 mm (¾–⅝ in)
- 6 T-connectors
- 6 elbow connectors
- 3 straight couplings
- rapid-drying epoxy adhesive
- used matchstick
- cross-connector
- funnel
- sand
- marbles

1 Using a pipe cutter, cut the copper pipe into sections as follows: 1 x 10 cm (4 in); 1 x 9 cm (3½ in); 3 x 6.5 cm (2½ in); 1 x 5 cm (2 in); 13 x 4 cm (1½ in); 2 x 3 cm (1¼ in).

2 To make the two outer candleholders, arrange the pieces you need in order, using 4 cm (1½ in) lengths of pipe: reducer, pipe, T-connector, pipe, elbow connector, pipe. For the central candleholder, use reducer, pipe, T-connector, pipe, straight coupling, pipe.

3 Glue in place, using a matchstick to apply the glue. Arrange the T-connectors so the holes are facing forwards.

4 To make the base, glue a T-connector, with the hole facing upwards, to a 6.5 cm (2½ in) pipe, then add an elbow connector, a 4 cm (1½ in) pipe, an elbow connector and another 4 cm (1½ in) pipe. Repeat on the other side of the T-connector. Now glue a 5 cm (2 in) pipe between the last two T-connectors. Add a 3 cm (1¼ in) pipe and a reducer to the holes in each of these T-connectors, which are pointing upwards. Glue this section into the front of the base.

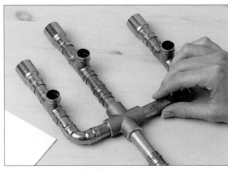

5 To make the central stand of the candelabra, glue the pipe and pieces as follows: 10 cm (4 in) pipe, straight coupling, 9 cm (3½ in) pipe, straight coupling, 6.5 cm (2½ in) pipe. Then glue the end of the last short length of pipe and the three candleholders into the cross-connector.

6 Fill the base of the candelabra with sand to act as "ballast" and make it very stable. Use a funnel to pour sand through the hole in one of the T-connectors at the base. Gently shake the base from time to time so the sand is evenly distributed.

7 Glue the top and bottom sections of the candelabra together. Provide support at the back and front to ensure that it dries in an upright position, with the T-connectors at the front parallel with the candle stand and candleholders. Glue coloured glass marbles on to the visible T-connector holes.

8 You can either leave the candelabra to weather naturally and mellow to an attractive finish or polish it regularly to maintain its shine.

candle collars

These lovely little collars are practical as well as decorative, as they catch any drips of hot wax that may run down the candle. Cut metal foil into stylized flower shapes, which can then be embossed with details such as dots and lines to make a relief design that will catch the light.

YOU WILL NEED

- paper and pencil, for the template
- 36 gauge (.005 in) aluminium foil
- protective gloves (optional)
- chinagraph pencil (china marker)
- small, pointed scissors
- soft cloth or old magazine
- empty ballpoint pen
- large droplet beads
- flat-headed silver pins (available from jewellery suppliers)
- wire-cutters
- small round-nosed pliers

For the circlets

- fine wire
- small beads

BELOW Candle collars or specially designed nightlight (tea-light) containers are a very safe way to hold slow-burning candles.

1 Copy the template at the back of the book. Place the template on a piece of foil and draw around it in chinagraph pencil (china marker). Cut out the flower and remove the central circle. Take care not to cut yourself on the sharp foil edges.

2 Place the foil flower, right side down, on a slightly yielding surface, such as a folded cloth or a magazine. Draw a circle at the base of the petals and draw veins on the petals with an empty ballpoint pen, pressing hard and evenly to make an impression.

3 Again using the ballpoint pen, make evenly spaced dots to fill the circle of the flower. Remove the soft surface, then make a small hole at the end of each petal with the tip of a scissor blade.

4 Thread droplet beads on to flat-headed silver pins. Trim the wire, leaving enough to attach to the flower. Thread a wire through the tip of each petal and bend over, using pliers.

5 Alternatively, make a delicate beaded circlet. Thread some small beads on to fine wire, then thread the wire through the hole in the petal and bend over. Continue to make loops of beaded wire all the way around the flower.

SAFETY HINTS
When you fit the collars to your chosen candlesticks, make sure that they curve up slightly at the edges in order to catch any dripping hot wax from the candles.

candleholders

. . . .

Weathered terracotta flowerpots make perfect containers for candles. Decorate the pots with collars of flowers or nuts, paint them with geometric border patterns or cover them with shells. Other original ideas include candle crowns and simply decorated gift boxes.

crowns

These metallic gold candleholders are very safe, as the flame is enclosed. As it burns down, pinprick patterns of light shine through the holes to give a very decorative effect. Choose your own design of geometric shapes, stylized flowers or simple stars.

YOU WILL NEED

- scissors
- 36 gauge (.005 in) copper foil
- sharp pencil
- ruler
- protective gloves (optional)
- round lid or coin
- bradawl (awl)
- old magazine or pile of newspapers
- small, pointed scissors
- brass paper fasteners

BELOW These delightful candleholders were made from soft drinks cans, pierced with a dressmaker's tracing wheel.

1 Cut a rectangle of foil 28 x 18 cm (11 x 7 in). Use a sharp pencil and ruler to draw a line across the length of the foil, dividing it in half. Then draw parallel diagonal lines across the width of the foil to make a lattice design. Using a round lid or a coin as a template, draw circles between the parallel lines along the top and the bottom edges.

2 Begin to punch regularly spaced holes along the pencilled lines, using a bradawl (awl). Punch a single hole in the centre of each circle and triangle. Place a magazine, a pile of newspapers or something similar, which will yield slightly and protect your work surface, underneath the foil.

3 Carefully cut along the top edge of the crown with scissors to leave a narrow border around the punched holes and make a scalloped rim.

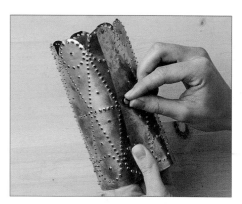

4 Gently bend the foil round so that the ends overlap slightly to form a cylinder. Make three corresponding marks on both pieces of foil where they meet and punch holes through them. Push a paper fastener through each set of holes to hold the foil in place, opening out the ends of the fastener on the inside.

JEWELLED CROWNS
Set glass nuggets for an extravagant crown. Cut a hole slightly smaller than the nugget, glue and press on.

candle collars

Turn ordinary tin cans into desirable objects by punching decorative patterns into the tin. To prevent the cans from denting as you work, they need to be lined with a solid material and cold, hard wax is ideal. As well as the cans keeping their shape, the wax also ensures a consistent size.

YOU WILL NEED

- empty tin cans
- can opener
- tape measure
- pencil
- scissors
- tracing paper
- measuring jug (cup)
- scales (scale)
- paraffin wax
- stearin (10% of quantity of wax)
- double boiler
- wooden spoon
- wax thermometer
- masking tape
- punch
- hammer
- bucket

2 For each design, fold the tracing paper in half widthways and draw a pattern on one half. Turn the folded paper over and trace the second half of the pattern so that it is symmetrical. Unfold the paper and redraw any faint lines.

4 When the wax is cold and hard, place a template around each can and hold in position with masking tape. Using a punch and hammer, gently but also firmly punch out the pattern on the can, following the template.

1 Soak the labels off the cans and then wash and dry the cans thoroughly inside and out, removing all traces of adhesive. Measure the height and circumference of each can. Cut out tracing paper templates to fit these measurements.

3 Fill each can with water and measure it. For every 100 ml (3½ fl oz) water you will need 90 g (3½ oz) cold paraffin wax. Melt the stearin in a double boiler. Add the paraffin wax and melt. Keep checking the temperature. When the temperature reaches 82°C (180°F), pour the wax into the cans and leave to cool and set completely.

5 When the entire pattern has been punched out, remove the tracing paper. Invert each can in a bucket and pour boiling water over it. This will soften the wax so that it slips out easily. Rinse the cans thoroughly with boiling water to remove any traces of wax. Remove the remaining ends of the cans with a can opener.

GARDEN flowers

Plant an instant border of giant flowers that look colourful by day and at night make an enchanting decoration for summer entertaining. The flowers are made of everyday materials, which are cheap and easy to find, and the stained-glass paint reflects the candlelight beautifully.

YOU WILL NEED

- permanent (magic) marker pens
- deep-sided foil pie dishes (pans)
- scissors
- stained-glass paints
- paintbrush
- small foil pie dishes (pans)
- brightly coloured foil from chocolate wrappers (optional)
- epoxy adhesive
- nightlights (tea-lights)
- large, flat-headed 2.5 cm (1 in) nails
- medium green garden canes (stakes)

BELOW Plant the candleholders in flowerbeds or in pots on a patio or simply use individual flowerheads to decorate place settings for an al fresco supper.

1 Draw the outline of rounded petals on the inside of a deep-sided foil pie dish (pan) with a permanent marker. Cut along the line with scissors to leave a flower shape.

2 Paint the flower, inside and out, with stained-glass paint in a bright, vibrant colour. Leave to dry thoroughly. Make more flowers, painting them in a variety of different colours.

3 Cover a small foil pie dish with coloured foil, smoothing out the foil and wrapping it over the rim to hold it securely in place. Alternatively, paint the container with stained-glass paint in a colour that will stand out against the large petals already painted.

4 Glue the metal surround from a nightlight (tea-light) into the container. Then, glue it inside the flower. Push a nail through the centre point of all three layers to hold them together.

5 Push the nail point into the pithy hollow at one end of a garden cane (stake). Add a blob of glue to the joint to hold it together. When the glue is dry, put the candle into the centre.

FOIL LEAVES
Mark and cut out a foil flan dish (large pie pan) into eight segments and scallop the edges. Attach a foil strip to the undersides with double-sided tape. Paint green. Tape to the stems.

PAINTED leaves

These folk-art leaf shapes make attractive candleholders, especially if you choose candles in colours to co-ordinate. The papier-mâché pulp dries to a hard finish, and several coats of gesso give a smooth surface for the paint, which is distressed slightly to give a worn, mellow look.

YOU WILL NEED

- paper and pencil, for the template
- corrugated cardboard
- craft knife and cutting mat
- metal bottle cap
- PVA (white) glue
- kitchen knife
- papier-mâché pulp
- newspaper
- wallpaper paste (without fungicide)
- gesso
- artist's paintbrushes
- acrylic paints
- fine sandpaper
- wax furniture polish
- soft cloth

1 Copy the leaf template at the back of the book and draw around it on to corrugated cardboard. Carefully cut out the shape using a craft knife. Place the bottle cap in the centre of the leaf and draw around it. Cut out the small circle, making sure that you are not cutting completely through, and remove the top layers of cardboard.

2 Remove pieces of cardboard or plastic lining from the inside of the bottle cap and check that it is clean. Then glue the bottle cap, upside-down, securely into the hollowed-out hole with PVA (white) glue and set aside to dry.

3 Using a kitchen knife, gradually build up the papier-mâché pulp on the leaf so that it is level with the edge of the bottle cap at the centre and slopes gently downward to the edges. Make a ridge along the middle of each lobe down to the tip of the leaf. Set the leaf aside for the pulp to dry.

4 Tear newspaper into small pieces and smear lightly on both sides with wallpaper paste. Paste these pieces over the surface of the leaf and down over the edges and underneath, so that it is covered on all sides. Set the leaf aside to dry completely.

5 Apply a coat of gesso with a paintbrush, covering the whole surface of the leaf. Set aside to dry completely. Apply two or three more coats of gesso, setting aside to dry thoroughly between each application.

6 Paint the leaf with acrylic paints and leave to dry. Emphasize the ridges on the leaf by alternating dark and light colours or shades.

7 Distress the paint finish by rubbing with fine sandpaper to take small areas back to the gesso. Wipe away any dust. Polish with wax polish, leave to harden for a while, then buff with a soft cloth.

candle design

This welcoming little candle pot uses a simple hay collar as the base for the decoration of walnuts, Brazil nuts and hazelnuts. Allow tendrils of moss to show through between the nuts in places to create a rich, overflowing effect. You can glaze the nuts to keep them shiny.

YOU WILL NEED

- hay
- reel (spool) wire, string or raffia
- glue gun and glue sticks
- small terracotta flowerpot
- moss
- walnuts, Brazil nuts and hazelnuts
- thick candle, to fit snugly inside the decorated pot

1 Glue a hay collar (see below) inside the top of the pot, then glue moss over it, allowing some to spill over the outside.

MAKING A HAY COLLAR

Scrunch a handful of hay into a sausage shape. Wind reel (spool) wire, string or raffia around it and tie to secure. Twist the binding around the hay at about 1 cm (½ in) intervals. Add more hay to build up a rope shape, keeping the binding very tight. Continue, keeping the width even, until you have the required length to sit inside the top of the pot. Fasten the end of the wire, string or raffia.

2 Arrange the nuts over the top of the collar, alternating the shapes and letting them overhang slightly. Glue them in place. Allow space for the candle to fit snugly in the centre.

3 Add the candle, holding it in place with plenty of damp moss pushed all around it.

D R I E D flowerpot

This striking design has a very modern look, with its use of massed flowers and vivid colour combinations. The candle is firmly supported by plastic foam (available from florist's suppliers), and the stems of the peonies and globe thistle are then pushed into the foam around it.

YOU WILL NEED

- knife
- block of florist's foam for dried flowers
- terracotta pot, 15 cm (6 in) diameter
- short, fat candle
- 10 dried deep pink peonies
- 15 stems dried small blue globe thistles
- wide ribbon
- scissors

1 Using a knife, cut a piece of florist's foam to size and wedge it firmly into the terracotta pot. Push the candle into the centre of the foam, keeping it straight.

2 Trim the peony stems to 4 cm (1½ in) and the globe thistle stems to 5 cm (2 in). Push the stems of the peonies into the foam. Then push the stems of the globe thistles into the foam among the peonies, ensuring that the heads of all the flowers are at the same level.

3 Wrap a ribbon around the pot, tie a bow and cut a "V" in the ends.

R U S T I C
candle

In this lovely candleholder, the muted colours of the dried flowers perfectly complement the cool cream church (ivory pillar) candle and the terracotta pot. The choice of dried materials includes aromatic bay leaves, scented lavender and small tied bundles of twigs.

You will need

- dried flowers, including foliage and grasses (6–8 varieties)
- scissors
- stub (floral) wires
- sharp knife
- block of florist's foam
- flowerpot
- hay or straw
- florist's tape
- church (ivory pillar) candle
- mossing (floral) pins (optional)
- moss

2 Turn down the end of the wire so that it is pointing towards the base of the stems. Now wrap the rest of the wire three or four times firmly around the stems to hold them together, covering the other end of the wire as you go and taking care not to apply much pressure that the stems break. Repeat these steps with the other bunches of flowers and foliage. You will need between six and eight bunches of each variety.

3 Trim the florist's foam to fit inside the flowerpot. Place it in the pot so that about 7.5 cm (3 in) of the foam stands proud above the rim. Pack hay or straw around the foam to provide a solid base for the candle.

4 Stick a piece of florist's tape all around the base of the candle. Hold three mossing (floral) pins or bent stub wires against the tape and tape over them to hold them in position.

5 Push the candle firmly into the florist's foam, then trim the foam, rounding off the corners neatly.

6 Add the wired bunches of flowers and foliage, sticking the stub wires into the florist's foam at an angle. Work with one variety at a time and place the bunches all round the candle to get an even balance of materials. If necessary, wire a few more small bunches together to fill any gaps.

7 Finally, attach some moss around the base of the candle with bent stub wires or mossing pins, making sure that it is pinned down well and that there are no loose wispy bits that might constitute a fire hazard.

1 Arrange the flowers and foliage in small bunches, with about four to six stems in each bunch. Cut the stems to about 13–15 cm (5–6 in) and hold one bunch of the flowers firmly in one hand. To wire them together, pass a stub (floral) wire behind the stems so that the wire and stems are at right angles to each other. Wrap about 4 cm (1½ in) of one end of the wire around the stems once. Do not cut the wire.

F L O R A L
pillar

This impressive construction is decorated with dried larkspur and lavender, a lovely combination for a summer party. The candle pillar is quite easy to make, but remember to only add as much material as you can comfortably handle, holding it in place with wire before adding more.

YOU WILL NEED

- glue gun and glue sticks
- small terracotta flowerpot
- tree trunk
- large terracotta flowerpot
- setting clay
- moss
- reel (spool) wire
- scissors
- dried larkspur
- dried lavender
- ruler
- stub (floral) wires or mossing (floral) pins
- tall candle

2 Tuck some of the moss into the base of the large flowerpot and wrap it around the base of the trunk, tying it in place with the reel (spool) wire. Keep the moss as even as possible and do not make the covering too thick.

4 Trim the larkspur and lavender to a length of approximately 13 cm (5 in). Starting at the top, tie the larkspur in placing using the reel wire.

1 Using a glue gun, glue the small terracotta flowerpot to the top of the tree trunk, making sure that it is completely level. Set the trunk in the large pot, using setting clay.

3 Continue wrapping the moss around the trunk and tying it in place until the entire trunk has been evenly covered, making sure that the area around the small flowerpot at the top of the trunk also has a good layer of moss.

5 Continue the process, adding the lavender and working down the whole length of the trunk. Each layer should cover the workings of the last. To cover the stem and the wire of the final layer at the base, wrap some green moss around them and hold in place with stub (floral) wires or mossing (floral) pins. Place the candle in the small flowerpot and hold in place with moss or glue.

WINTER box

This rich display of nuts and dried fruits surrounding a tall candle would look very handsome on a dark polished sideboard or table. The base is a plain cardboard box, which is transformed by covering it with preserved (dried) leaves glued in place. The loose raffia bow is purely decorative.

YOU WILL NEED

- knife
- block of florist's foam
- cardboard box
- glue gun and glue sticks
- selection of preserved (dried) leaves
- natural raffia
- scissors
- reindeer moss
- tall candle
- selection of nuts and dried fruits
- dried red chillies
- stub (floral) wires

BELOW Try a rectangular-shaped box, filled with old pots and dried twigs and flowers.

1 Using a craft or other sharp knife, trim the florist's foam block to the shape of the box. Apply some glue to the base of the box, then push the foam firmly into it. Try to create a good, tight fit, as this will ensure that the box keeps its shape and that the candle and other materials are firmly positioned.

2 Spread a little glue on the back of each leaf and press it firmly on to the side of the box. If the leaves are not large enough to cover the depth of the box, start the first row of leaves at the top and cover the bottom of the previous row with the next row. Place the top row of leaves so that they extend well above the rim of the box.

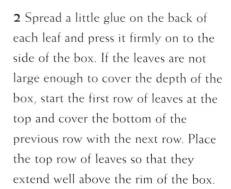

3 Wrap strands of raffia around the box and tie it in a large loose bow. Trim all the leaves that extend over the base of the box so that the box will stand flat. Take care not to split the leaves.

4 Arrange some reindeer moss inside the box around the edge, leaving the centre clear for the other decorations.

5 Holding the candle firmly, push it into the foam in the centre of the box to make a hole. Remove the candle and put a little glue into the hole, then replace the candle.

6 Arrange the nuts and dried fruits decoratively in the box, keeping the most attractive items, such as the dried oranges, until last. Make the dried red chillies into small bunches and tie with stub (floral) wires). Tie with raffia to cover the wire, then gently push the ends of the wire through the fruit and chillies into the foam.

lanterns

■ ■ ■ ■

Everyone loves the warm-coloured light radiating from pumpkin lanterns and, because the candle is enclosed, they are quite safe. Glass lanterns are also magical, using ordinary jam jars to great effect. In contrast, hand-made paper lanterns have a delicate, fragile beauty.

CUT-OUT
paper lanterns

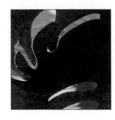

Hand-made paper makes lovely lanterns, and there is a wide range to choose from. In these lanterns the candlelight shines through the Matisse-style leaf cut-outs. In the triangular-shaped lantern, the shapes are only partly cut, so the glow of the candle is cast upwards.

YOU WILL NEED

- paper and pencil, for the template
- thick hand-made paper, approximately 20 x 30 cm (8 x 12 in) – 1 sheet for each lantern
- tracing paper
- craft knife and cutting mat
- double-sided adhesive (cellophane) tape
- scissors
- metal ruler
- kitchen knife

3 Place double-sided tape along one short side of the hand-made paper. Peel away the backing.

4 Curve the paper into a cylinder and press the overlap firmly together.

1 For the cylindrical lantern, scale up the template for this lantern at the back of the book to fit a sheet of hand-made paper. Transfer to tracing paper.

2 Using a craft knife and cutting mat, carefully cut around the traced outlines.

5 To make the triangular lantern, scale up the template for this lantern and trace the design lines on to a sheet of hand-made paper. Using a craft knife and cutting mat, carefully cut along the solid outlines of the motifs only.

6 Lightly crease each motif along the dotted line so that the shapes protrude a little from the lantern.

7 On the reverse side of the paper, score along the vertical dotted fold lines using a ruler and the back of a kitchen knife.

8 Crease along the scored lines then bend the lantern into a triangular shape, securing the overlap with a strip of double-sided tape. Make sure both the lanterns stand up securely.

JAPANESE
paper shades

The natural textures of hand-made Japanese paper are ideally suited to the soft glow of candlelight. Begin with a simply folded cylinder, then advance to the more elaborate petal shape illustrated opposite. Always be careful with paper shades, and never leave lighted candles

YOU WILL NEED

- paper and pencil, for the template
- hand-made Japanese paper
- scissors
- masking tape
- bradawl (awl)
- willow twig
- double-sided adhesive (cellophane) tape
- craft knife and cutting mat
- strip of natural pine or thin card (card stock)

1 To make the simple shade, scale up the simple shade template for this project at the back of the book using paper and pencil. Transfer the lantern shape on to hand-made Japanese paper. Make faint pencil marks to indicate the positions of the holes needed for the fastener and then carefully cut out the shade with scissors.

2 Place a small tab of masking tape on the back of the hand-made paper at each hole position, to act as an extra reinforcement for when they are being cut out.

3 Using a bradawl (awl), pierce small holes where indicated on the template.

4 Cut a short length of willow twig. Bend the paper into a cylinder and match up the holes. Insert the twig to hold the shade together.

5 To make the petal shade, scale up the double petal shade templates at the back of the book and draw on Japanese paper. Cut them out, marking the overlap and fastener slits with a pencil.

6 Reinforce the back of each slit position with masking tape, then lay the two pieces flat, overlapping where indicated. Join together with double-sided tape. Make slits where indicated on the template, using a craft knife.

7 Cut a fairly thin, elongated triangular fastener from a strip of pine or thin card (card stock) and insert it into the slits.

8 For a cylinder, use double-sided tape for the overlap and bend over the petals.

J A C K
o' lantern

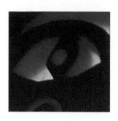

It is fun to make individual characters with traditional Hallowe'en lanterns. This fierce Jack o'lantern has a splendid curling moustache, giving him a striking appearance. The nose and eyebrows are cut in one line, and a pumpkin hat sets him apart from the average run of lanterns.

YOU WILL NEED

- water-soluble crayon
- large pumpkin
- kitchen knife
- spoon
- fine black pen
- craft knife
- bradawl (awl)
- lino-cutting tool (linoleum knife)
- small yellow pumpkin for the hat
- nightlight (tea-light)

1 Draw a circle 9 cm (3½ in) diameter on the top of the pumpkin. Cut out and scoop out the seeds and flesh with a spoon, leaving a shell 1 cm (½ in) thick.

3 Using a craft knife, carefully cut the nose and eyebrows in a single, curving line. Cut out the whites of the eyes, leaving the iris intact. Use a bradawl (awl) to make a hole in the centre of each eye.

5 To make the hat, cut out a circle in the base of the small pumpkin with a sharp kitchen knife. Scoop out the flesh and seeds to leave a hollow shell. Draw decorative scrolls all around the outside of the pumpkin shell with the crayon.

2 Grasp the pumpkin shell firmly with one hand to stop it rolling about and draw the facial features on one side with a black pen. Apply the eyebrows and nose in a continuous line, then add the eyes with pupils and irises, a long, curly moustache and a large grinning mouth with chunky teeth showing.

4 Use a lino-cutting tool (linoleum knife) to cut out the moustache. Cut the space between the grinning teeth with the craft knife. Cut these out carefully as you do not want any teeth to break off.

6 Using the craft knife, carefully cut the scrolls into curling slits. Place the nightlight (tea-light) in the large pumpkin, then place the hat on top. Besides decorating the hat, the slits are necessary to allow plenty of air through the cut-out design, since otherwise the candle may go out.

pumpkin

Delicate tracery looks magnificent on a rich orange pumpkin, especially when the light shines through the thin shell. Draw the curly lines and circles freehand to echo the wavy lines around the lid and the shape of the pumpkin itself, then cut out with lino-cutting tools (linoleum knives).

YOU WILL NEED

- fibre-tip pen
- pumpkin
- pumpkin saw or small saw
- kitchen knife
- spoon
- lino-cutting tools (linoleum knives)
- nightlight (tea-light)

3 Draw an all-over tracery pattern on the skin of the pumpkin, working circles and curlicues freehand.

BELOW Use tools of a different thickness to cut out the lines and curls for a varying effect.

4 Use lino-cutting tools (linoleum knives) in various thicknesses to cut out the pattern. Try out the nightlight (tea-light) to check that the light shines through. If not, scrape away a little more of the inside of the shell.

1 Draw a wavy line around the top of the pumpkin to mark the edge of the lid. Cut around this with a small saw. Use a sharp kitchen knife to cut out quite a large circle in the centre of the lid.

2 Scoop out all the seeds and flesh with a spoon. Scrape away the inside to leave a thin shell.

FOLK-ART lantern

Decorate a rich golden pumpkin with a wide border of traditional country motifs. Holes punched through the pumpkin allow the candlelight inside to shine through. Templates for the two cockerel (rooster) designs and the star are given elsewhere in the book.

YOU WILL NEED
- water-soluble crayon
- pumpkin
- pumpkin saw or small saw
- spoon
- lino-cutting tool (linoleum knife)
- craft knife
- flat-edged tool
- paper and pencil, for the templates
- dressmaking pins
- fine black pen
- bradawl (awl)
- nightlight (tea-light)

2 Using a craft knife, cut two borders of small triangles freehand adjoining the two lines, without cutting all the way through. Lift the shapes out using a flat-edged tool.

4 When the complete design has been traced, remove the templates and carefully cut out the shapes, slicing through the shell of the pumpkin with the craft knife.

1 Using a crayon, draw a circle on the top of the pumpkin and cut out with a small saw to ensure that there will be sufficient air for the nightlight (tea-light) to burn. Using a spoon, remove the seeds and flesh to leave a fairly thin shell. Draw two parallel lines around the body of the pumpkin about 10 cm (4 in) apart. Cut along the lines, but not completely through them, with a lino-cutting tool (linoleum knife).

3 Trace the two cockerel (rooster) and the star templates from the back of the book and enlarge them, if necessary, to make a frieze around the middle of the pumpkin shell. Pin them in position and draw around them with a black pen. Alternate the two cockerels (roosters) around the lantern, with a star in between them each time.

5 Using a bradawl (awl), make a random decoration by piercing holes around the shapes, as shown. Place a nightlight (tea-light) inside the lantern.

VARIATION
Make up your own templates for personalized pumpkin lanterns.

squash

A simple pattern of large round holes creates a very modern effect, especially if you choose to work with an unusual pale green squash. The holes are created with a drill bit, twisting it back through each hole in an anti-clockwise (counterclockwise) direction to avoid damaging the skin.

You will need

- water-soluble crayon
- pale green squash
- pumpkin saw or small saw
- spoon
- woodcarving tool
- 2.5 cm (1 in) drill bit
- nightlight (tea-light)

1 Using a crayon, draw a circle on the top of the squash about 9 cm (3½ in) diameter. Cut out, using a small saw. Scoop out the seeds with a spoon. Using a woodcarving tool, carefully chip away at the flesh until the shell is no more than 2 cm (¾ in) thick.

2 Holding a drill bit in your hand, pierce through the shell using a pushing and twisting action. Once the bit is through, remove it by twisting it back in an anti-clockwise (counterclockwise) direction. Repeat to make a regular pattern of holes. If you wish, you can use different-size drill bits to vary the pattern. Place a nightlight (tea-light) inside the lantern.

BABY
pumpkin

A group of these small, characterful lanterns would create a magical effect at an outdoor party in the early evening, or as an unusual Christmas decoration indoors. Decorate each one differently with zigzags, slits and scrolls, all carved with a craft knife.

YOU WILL NEED
- fine black pen
- small pumpkins or squash
- craft knife
- teaspoon
- nightlights (tea-lights)

1 Using a pen, draw a circle on the base of each pumpkin. Cut out the shape, using a craft knife. Scoop out the flesh with a teaspoon.

2 Draw zigzags on one pumpkin and cut away with the craft knife. The slits should be 5 mm (¼ in) wide in the middle, tapering to points at both ends.

3 Draw and cut straight slits on another pumpkin. Draw a scroll design on a third pumpkin, then carefully cut it away using the craft knife. Light the nightlights (tea-lights) and place the baby pumpkin lanterns on top.

VARIATION
An attractive feature of a small pumpkin is that since the hole is in the base, the stalks are left intact.

O V A L
squash

Small oval squash, such as Yellow Acorn or Golden Acorn, make unusual lanterns, and the soft buttermilk shades of their skins are very attractive. This design is simply rows of holes pierced along the natural ridges of the squash with a bradawl (awl), through which the light shines.

YOU WILL NEED

- water-soluble crayon
- small oval ridged squash
- kitchen knife
- large spoon
- teaspoon
- bradawl (awl)
- nightlight (tea-light)

1 Using a crayon, mark a large square on one side of the squash. Cut out and remove this part of the squash wall, using a kitchen knife. When it is laid on its side, this will be the bottom.

2 First using a large spoon and then the teaspoon, scrape out the seeds and flesh, making sure you clean out very thoroughly along the inside of the ridges. The shell should be about 1 cm (½ in) thick.

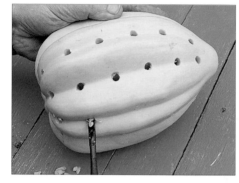

3 Using a bradawl (awl), make neat lines of regularly spaced holes along each of the furrows of the squash. Light the nightlight (tea-light) and place the squash lantern over it, positioned on its cut side.

G L A S S
pots

Jam jars make excellent lanterns. Here they are coated with stained-glass paints, then decorated with swirling patterns in outline paint. Stained-glass paints come in a range of rich translucent colours. Collect a mixture of jars with flat faceted sides or other unusual features.

YOU WILL NEED

- clean glass jam jars
- flat bristle artist's paintbrush, about 1 cm (½ in) wide
- stained-glass paints
- outline paint
- nightlights (tea-lights)

1 Paint the outside of a jam jar with undiluted stained-glass paint. Be generous with the amount, but avoid drips.

2 When dry, squeeze the outline paint directly from the tube nozzle on to the jar in your desired pattern. Let the paint flow evenly. Leave to dry for 3 days until the paint has set hard. Insert a nightlight (tea-light) or candle.

glass lanterns

These lovely little lanterns are made by covering the surface of drinking tumblers with a colourful mosaic of stained glass. Cut the mosaic pieces yourself by carefully measuring the stained glass, then scoring the lines with a glass cutter. The pieces are stuck with invisible ultra-violet glue.

YOU WILL NEED

- permanent black (magic) pen
- metal ruler
- stained glass in blue, green, red and yellow
- glass cutter
- heavy-based glass tumbler
- ultra-violet glue
- spatula and bowl
- tile grout
- black acrylic paint
- rubber (latex) gloves
- sponge scourer
- nightlight (tea-light)

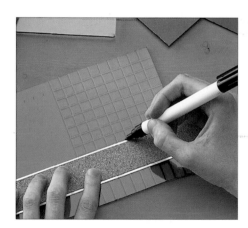

1 Using a permanent black pen and a metal ruler, mark a grid of 1 cm (½ in) squares on a piece of the stained glass.

2 Cut the glass into strips 1 cm (½ in) wide by scoring it with a glass cutter, using the metal ruler as a guide. Gently tap the underside of the score line with the hammer end of the glass cutter, then carefully snap the glass apart between both thumbs. If it is difficult to snap, tap with the hammer end again.

3 Score the glass strip into 1 cm (½ in) squares. Turn the strip over so the score lines are face down on the worktop and gently tap each score line with the hammer end of the glass cutter. The glass should break easily into squares. Repeat these three steps with the other sheets of stained glass.

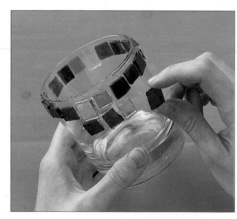

4 Using ultra-violet glue (which will not show when the candle is lit), stick the mosaic pieces around the glass tumbler, working from the top to the bottom. Leave a gap of 2 mm (¹⁄₁₆ in) between the squares to allow for grouting.

5 In a bowl, mix 30 ml (2 tbsp) tile grout with 25 ml (5 tsp) cold water and a 5 cm (2 in) length of black acrylic paint. Stir until it forms a smooth, dark grey paste. If your skin is sensitive, it is a good idea to wear rubber (latex) gloves to protect your hands. Using a spatula, press the grout mixture well into the gaps between the mosaic pieces. Remove excess grout with the spatula. Leave to dry completely.

6 When the lantern is dry, use a damp sponge scourer to clean any remaining smears of grout from the surface of the mosaic pieces. Place a nightlight (tea-light) inside the lantern.

chandeliers

∎ ∎ ∎ ∎

These elegant shapes from a past age are still a lovely way to display candles. Simple materials, such as wire and foil, can be moulded into graceful coils that reflect the candlelight. Materials such as papier-mâché and weathered wood give quite different sculptural effects.

COILED wire sconce

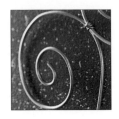

Scrolling coils of pale galvanized wire make a lovely, delicate sconce. Individual lengths of wire are bent into shape with pliers, following the template at the back of the book. Fine wire is then used like thread to bind the pieces together and make up the finished design.

YOU WILL NEED

- paper and pencils, for the template
- tape measure
- wire-cutters
- 3 mm (⅛ in) gauge galvanized wire
- long-nosed pliers
- fine galvanized wire
- clear adhesive tape
- candle

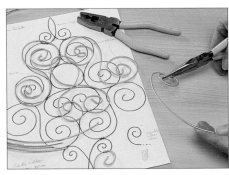

1 Scale up the template at the back of the book to the finished size required and draw it on a piece of paper. Using the wire-cutters, cut the 3 mm (⅛ in) wire into the following lengths: 2 x 30 cm (12 in) for the top hanger and lower coils; 1 x 50 cm (20 in) for the centre piece; 4 x 55 cm (21½ in) for the side pieces; 1 x 80 cm (32 in) for the candle-holder.

2 Using long-nosed pliers, carefully bend each length of wire smoothly and evenly to fit the relevant coiled shape on the paper template.

3 Take the top hanger piece and wind the fine wire around the cross-over point by hand. Trim the wire and take the ends to the back of the sconce. Turn the shape over and twist the ends of the fine wire together securely, then snip off any excess with the pliers. Wire all the seams in this way.

4 Secure two of the side pieces in position under the hanger with small tabs of adhesive tape at the points indicated on the template. The tape will hold the coils steady while you are working. Make strong wire seams at the taped points, using fine wire.

5 Tape the centre piece into position between the two side pieces, then wind the fine wire around the small triangular shape in the centre. Tape the other pieces into position and make small wire seams to secure them, winding a short piece of fine wire around three times. Secure the ends by twisting them together at the back.

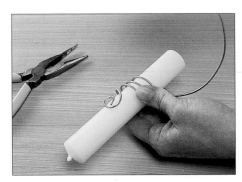

6 Make the candle-holder with the remaining length of 3 mm (⅛ in) wire. Begin with a small decorative spiral, then wind the wire around the candle about five times.

7 Bend the end of the candle-holder wire underneath the coil across the base, then into an elongated hook shape at the back. Hook the holder on to the sconce and wire securely in place.

wall flowers

These attractive sconces are ingeniously made out of a variety of copper parts, including a mould from a kitchenware shop, pipe and attachments from a plumber's merchant and a small car mirror. The deep rich tones of the copper and the mirrored flower centre reflect the candle's light.

YOU WILL NEED

- terracotta-coloured and standard epoxy putty
- small copper mousse mould
- copper reducer to fit pipes 16 mm to 10 mm (⅝ in to ½ in) (available from plumber's merchants)
- paper and pencil, for the template
- thin card (card stock)
- scissors or tin snips
- .005 in thick (36 gauge) copper foil
- copper-coloured permanent (magic) pen
- protective gloves (optional)
- craft knife
- pliers
- self-adhesive-backed round mirror
- bending spring, to fit the copper pipe
- thin copper pipe, 8 mm (⅜ in) diameter and 30 cm (12 in) long
- wooden rolling pin
- drill or bradawl (awl)
- epoxy adhesive
- used matchstick
- heavy-duty double-sided sticky pads
- copper foil adhesive (cellophane) tape

1 Mix equal parts of the terracotta-coloured and standard epoxy putties and knead together well until they have become thoroughly blended and are evenly copper-coloured. Place a good-sized blob of the epoxy putty on the base of the copper mousse mould, then push the reducer into the putty to join them together. Set aside and leave to dry out completely.

2 Copy the template at the back of the book and then transfer it on to thin card (card stock). Mark the area of copper foil to be used to make the flower, then draw around the template on to the copper foil, using a permanent marker. Carefully cut out the flower shape with sharp scissors or tin snips. Cut out the centre circle carefully with a craft knife, keeping it for later use. Take care not to cut yourself on the sharp foil edges.

3 Gently score lines down the centre of each copper petal with the craft knife and then crease the metal lightly along these lines. Gather and pleat the foil loosely around the central circle, using pliers where necessary, until the flower is three-dimensional and the petals are realistically cupped.

4 Colour the edge of the mirror with the marker pen so it matches the copper. Place the copper circle behind the flower centre. Peel the covering off the back of the adhesive pad on the mirror and attach the mirror to the copper circle so that the flower is neatly sandwiched between them. For an extra decorative feature, before you fasten the mirror in position, you can lightly burnish the foil petal edges by holding the flower with tongs over a flame.

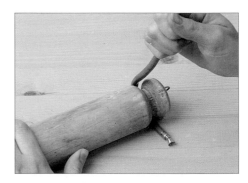

5 Insert the bending spring inside the thin copper pipe. Hold a wooden rolling pin with handles steady with one hand. Then bend the pipe about a quarter of the way along its length around one handle. Carefully bend the pipe until it forms a smoothly curved hook, then remove the spring.

6 Flatten the end of the longer part of the pipe by squeezing it evenly with pliers to form a flat surface on which to attach the flower. Use a drill or bradawl (awl) to make a hole 1 cm (½ in) from the end of the flattened part.

7 Apply epoxy adhesive to the reducer with the matchstick and stick it to the round end of the length of copper pipe. Leave to set. Stick the flower to the flattened part of the pipe with sticky pads, leaving the hole free for hanging. Cover the seams with strips of copper foil tape to neaten the back.

sconce

This quirky candleholder has a solid base of corrugated cardboard, covered with papier-mâché. In the final layer, torn pages from books are left visible as part of the decoration. Delicate touches of gold glint in the candlelight, and curls of twisted wire join the upright to the base.

YOU WILL NEED

- paper and pencil, for the template
- ruler
- fibre-tip pen
- heavy corrugated cardboard
- strong scissors
- masking tape
- PVA (white) glue
- brush for glue
- galvanized wire
- pliers (optional)
- newspaper
- wallpaper paste
- mixing bowl
- old book
- white emulsion (latex) paint
- paint-mixing container
- gold wax crayon
- acrylic spray varnish
- nightlight (tea-light) in metal container
- strong clear glue
- small mirror

1 Scale up the template at the back of the book and draw in fibre-tip pen on corrugated cardboard, with a heart shape too. Three layers are used for the back (pointed, if you like) and base.

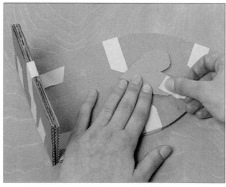

2 Cut out and stick the layers for the back and base together with masking tape, then tape them at right angles. Tape the heart shape to the upper back section, leaving room for the mirror.

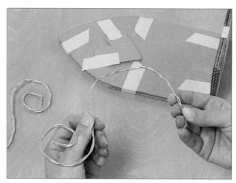

3 Seal the cardboard with a coat of diluted PVA (white) glue and set aside to dry. Meanwhile, twist two lengths of galvanized wire together, then, using pliers or your fingers, carefully bend them into a smooth, curly S-shape that will fit neatly between the back and the base of the sconce. Twist two more lengths of galvanized wire together and bend the second pair into an S-shape that exactly matches the first.

4 Once the sconce is dry, tape the supports firmly to the back and base. Tear newspaper into 2.5 cm (1 in) strips and soak in wallpaper paste. Cover the sconce in four layers of papier-mâché. Tear up a few pages from an old book to use for the final layer.

5 Leave to dry completely, then paint all over with a thin wash of diluted white emulsion (latex) paint. Some of the print from the pages of the old book will show through. When dry, colour the heart gold and add an all-over pattern of spots with a gold wax crayon.

6 Spray the sconce with acrylic varnish. Apply a few coats to give a good finish, leaving it to dry between them.

7 Decorate the nightlight (tea-light) container with white emulsion (latex) paint and gold wax crayon to match the sconce and glue it in the middle of the base. Using strong, clear glue, stick a small mirror to the inside lower back of the sconce.

wall hanging

This rustic wall sconce is easy to make, and its simplicity is a great part of its charm. Find an interesting piece of weathered driftwood, or any similar rugged wood with character. Decorate it with your own pattern of brass- and black-headed upholstery nails hammered into the sconce.

YOU WILL NEED

- saw
- long piece of driftwood
- hammer
- brass-headed and black-headed upholstery nails
- wood glue
- fine, long nails
- short, fat candle

1 Saw through the wood to make a short shelf and a longer upright. Hammer a line of nails in the centre of the upright.

2 Form different shapes such as arrows, and crosses, alternating the brass and black nails as part of your design.

3 Apply wood glue to the sawn edge of the shelf. Place the two pieces of wood together at right angles, then hammer fine nails through the back of the upright into the base to join them together securely. Stand a short fat candle on the shelf, which must be wide enough for the candle wax to spill directly on to the bare wood.

HOLLY chandelier

For the winter festivities, decorate the rim of a wire chandelier with a garland of variegated holly. Choose young branches of holly with small offshoots that will give bulk and depth to make a rounded garland shape. Thornless holly is, of course, much easier to work with.

YOU WILL NEED

- newspaper
- large pine cones
- antique gold spray paint
- wire hanging basket
- secateurs (pruners)
- variegated holly
- florist's reel (spool) wire

1 Cover your work surface with newspaper, then spray the pine cones with antique gold paint. Leave to dry before placing them in the wire basket.

2 Using secateurs (pruners), cut individual branches of holly and attach them around the rim of the basket with reel (spool) wire.

3 Again using reel wire, fasten a generous sprig of holly to hang below the bottom of the basket.

HELPFUL HINT
You may be lucky enough to find an old chandelier in a junk shop or at a flea market that you can use here.

hanging

This novel chandelier is inexpensively made out of two metal flan (tart) rings, painted green to give a rustic effect. Bands of rusty tin secure the candle-holders, which are simply small drinking glasses. Colour the glasses if you wish by painting them with stained glass paints.

YOU WILL NEED
- 2 flan (tart) rings, 25 cm (10 in) and 18 cm (7 in) in size
- tape measure
- pencil
- bradawl (awl)
- green water-based paint
- paintbrush
- thin card (card stock)
- scissors
- 9 small glasses
- old tin, preferably rusty
- tin snips
- protective gloves (optional)
- 18 paper fasteners
- epoxy adhesive
- metal chain, preferably brass
- wire-cutters
- 10 "S" links
- round-nosed pliers
- 9 nightlights (tea-lights)

1 Measure the circumference of the large ring and divide into six equal sections, marking each with a line. With a bradawl (awl), make two holes in the centre of the ring, 1.5 cm (⅝ in) on either side of each line. Repeat with the small ring, but you divide it into three and make only three pairs of holes.

2 Paint both rings, inside and out with a coat of green water-based paint. Leave the paint to dry thoroughly.

3 Make holes to hang the chains on. Punch three equidistant holes close to the top edge of the large ring. Punch three holes close to the top edge, and three directly below them but close to the bottom edge of the small ring.

4 To make the glass holders, make a template from thin card (card stock) for the tin bands. For glasses with 18 cm (7 in) circumference, draw them 20 cm (8 in) long and 2 cm (¾ in) deep with curved sides and rounded corners. Cut nine bands out of tin using tin snips. It is advisable to wear protective gloves.

5 Make a hole with a bradawl at both ends of each band – they should be centred and 5 mm (¼ in) from the ends.

6 Bend each band just over 1 cm (½ in) from its ends and curve the central part around a glass to shape it.

7 Place one band over a pair of holes on the large ring. Push a paper fastener through each hole. Apply epoxy adhesive to the underside of the band. Flatten the paper fasteners on the inside of the ring. Attach the other holders in the same way. Check that the glasses fit into the holders and do not fall through.

8 Cut three equal lengths of chain and attach "S" links to each end. Open the link with pliers and attach the chains to the three holes on the top rim of the large ring. Attach the other ends to the holes on the lower edge of the small ring. Cut three more equal lengths of chain and attach them to the top edge of the small ring, with "S" links.

9 Thread the three chains at the top edge of the small ring through an "S" link. Attach a length of chain for hanging. Paint over the fasteners. Insert the nightlights (tea-lights).

decoration

Embellish a plain candelabra with a garland of shiny metal foil oak leaves. The leaves are threaded on to soft wire, which is easy to bend and will twine naturally around the base shape. Three shades of metal foil – aluminium, copper and bronze – give extra interest.

You will need

- paper and pencil, for template
- thin card (card stock)
- scissors
- .003 in thick (40 gauge) aluminium, copper and bronze foil
- chinagraph pencil (china marker)
- small, pointed scissors
- protective gloves (optional)
- dressmaker's tracing wheel
- magazine or pile of old newspapers
- bradawl (awl)
- 1 mm (1/32 in) diameter soft copper wire
- plain chandelier

1 Copy the template of the oak leaf at the back of the book and transfer it on to thin card (cardstock). Cut out the template and place on a piece of copper foil. Draw around the template with a chinagraph pencil (china marker).

2 Remove the template and cut the leaf shape out of the copper foil with small scissors. (Small embroidery scissors are ideal for this.) Take care not to cut yourself on the sharp edges of the foil; you may prefer to wear protective gloves. Take your time and trim away any rough edges as necessary.

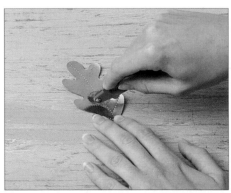

3 To create veins on the foil leaf, run a dressmaker's tracing wheel evenly down the centre to produce pinprick lines. Then, make small diagonal veins from the central rib to the edges of the leaf. You will have to press quite hard to make clear impressions in the foil. It may help to work on a slightly yielding surface, such as a magazine or pile of old newspapers.

4 Make more leaves out of the three different foils in the same way and mark them with veins. Punch a hole with a bradawl (awl) in the stalk end of each leaf. Don't make the hole too big – just large enough to thread the leaf on to the wire. Cut a length of wire long enough to wind around one of the arms of the chandelier. Thread the leaves on to the wire, alternating the metals.

5 Twist the wire around one arm of the chandelier to make a secure starting point. Wind the wire around the chandelier, with a leaf every 8–10 cm (3–4 in), then secure the end tightly. Continue until the chandelier is completely decorated. Hang three or four leaves under the centre.

TASSELLED chandelier

Transform a cheap or tarnished metal chandelier by binding the entire shape with string; a simple shape is easiest to work on. Decorate the candleholders and the bottom of the chandelier with delightful tassels made of paper cord, which seem to have a life of their own.

YOU WILL NEED

- scissors
- corrugated cardboard
- paper cord
- craft knife
- gold thread
- beads
- PVA (white) glue
- large ball of string
- simple metal chandelier
- spray paint (optional)

1 First. make the tassels – one to hang below each candleholder. Cut two rectangles of corrugated cardboard – the length should be the length you want the tassels to be. Put the two together and wind paper cord around them – the more cord you use, the thicker the tassels will be. Thread a piece of paper cord between the rectangles, pull up and tie tightly at one end to make the top of the tassel. Cut through the cord at the other end with a craft knife.

2 Remove the cardboard and bind the tassel with gold thread 3 cm (1¼ in) below the top, tying the ends tightly. Slip another length of gold thread through the top of the tassel, thread a bead on to it and tie a knot to hold in place. Make a tassel for each candle-holder in the same way and a slightly larger one to hang from the bottom of the chandelier.

3 Starting at the central core of the chandelier, glue the end of the string to one of the arms. Wind the string around the arm, gradually working towards the holder and completely covering the metal. When you reach the holder, cut the string and glue the end in place, holding it firmly until it has stuck.

4 Cut a small strip of cardboard to fit around each candleholder. Glue in place, then wind string around from the bottom to the top of the cardboard until it is covered. Cut the string and glue the end at the top. Cover all the arms and candleholders in the same way, followed by the central core. If the chandelier has push-in candle-holders, give them a coat of spray paint and glue in position.

5 If the chandelier has a weighted ball underneath, glue the gold thread holding the bead at the top of the large tassel around it. Beginning at the bead, spiral and glue string around the ball to cover. Hang the chandelier in position, then carefully tie or glue a tassel underneath each candleholder.

WINTER hanging

This highly original winter decoration is based on a willow or hop vine garland ring. Decorate it with starfish-covered oranges, lightly spray-painted gold to show their natural textures. As a final decoration, frost the garland and ropes with a little gold paint and glue on a few starfish.

YOU WILL NEED

- knife
- dried oranges
- small screwdriver
- stub (floral) wires
- glue gun and glue sticks
- sphagnum moss
- small starfish
- gold spray paint
- rope
- garland ring
- 4 florist's candle-holders
- 4 candles

1 Cut the oranges in half and make a hole in each half with a screwdriver. Push the two ends of a bent stub (floral) wire through the hole to make a hanging loop. Turn the orange over and bend the ends of the wire up, to prevent the loop from falling out.

2 Coat the inside of each orange with some glue. Push sphagnum moss carefully into the space, so that it is completely filled.

3 Hold a starfish on an orange. Place glue on the moss and around the edge of the orange, where the starfish touches it. Hold the starfish in place until the glue sets. Dab a little glue on two or three more starfish and place them on the top and sides of the orange.

4 Bend the top and bottom of a stub wire, hang the orange on one end and spray it gently with gold paint. Use the paint so that it provides a frosting, rather than a solid colour, letting a little of the orange colour show through. Repeat for the other oranges.

5 Tie four lengths of rope firmly to the ring so that the chandelier hangs horizontally. The length of rope will depend on the final hanging position, so at this stage keep the ropes fairly long and adjust them later. Push a handful of sphagum moss on to the ring between two ropes. Make a small hole in the centre with your fingers.

6 Using the glue gun, put glue in the hole made in the moss and push a candleholder into it, making sure that it is completely straight. You may find it helpful to put the candle into the holder to check. Hang the oranges on the ring when the ring is in its final position.

displays

■ ■ ■

For any occasion, a display of candles and flowers creates the right effect. Many leaves and berries are also decorative, their glossy, rich colours complementing the cool wax candles. Two lovely ideas for Advent and a Christmas mantelpiece celebrate the festive season.

candle rings

Small dried roses make a very romantic decoration around the base of a candle. Glue pairs of roses in different colours alternately around the cane ring, angling the heads so that they face outwards. Check the shape regularly as you work to make sure it looks evenly balanced.

YOU WILL NEED

- glue gun and glue sticks
- titancia moss
- small cane ring
- scissors
- dried roses
- extra dried flowers and foliage
  (eg bupleurum)
- candle

1 Using the glue gun, attach a light covering of moss to the cane ring. Try to make sure that no glue is visible.

2 Cut the roses from their stems and glue them into place. Position them to maintain a symmetry in design. Work on one side of the ring and then the other to get the balance right.

3 Fill the spaces with extra roses and moss, using glue. Make sure the hole remaining in the middle is large enough to hold the candle. Fill any remaining gaps with moss.

GARLAND of hops

The subtle green tones of hop flowers team beautifully with a rich golden beeswax candle in this attractive table centrepiece. Hops retain their translucent beauty when dried, but the stems, or bines, become brittle and difficult to work with so the flowers are best for decoration.

You will need

- large, sharp knife
- florist's foam ball, 10 cm (4 in) diameter
- saucer
- thick beeswax candle
- scissors
- dried hops
- bay leaf sprigs

1 With a large sharp knife, cut the florist's foam ball in half, then cut a 2.5 cm (1 in) thick slice off one side.

2 Place the cut florist's foam in a saucer. Push the candle gently through the centre of the foam.

3 Cut the hop flowers off the stems, leaving them in their clusters where possible. Push the stalks into the foam to cover it completely.

4 Push the sprigs of bay leaves into the foam, placing them at regular intervals around the ring. Extinguish the candle before it reaches the garland.

display

Make the most of the first "Christmas roses", or hellebores, with this enchanting display. The blue-green of the eucalyptus leaves is the perfect foil for the creamy white of the hellebore flowers and church (ivory pillar) candles, and they have a distinctive fresh smell.

YOU WILL NEED

- large, sharp knife
- large florist's foam ball
- plate
- 4 slim church (ivory pillar) candles
- scissors
- eucalyptus
- white hellebore flowers

1 Using a large knife, cut the florist's foam ball in half (or slice off a section if larger) to fit the plate. Soak the foam in water and leave to drain. (Soaking the foam in water ensures that the fresh flowers will last for several days and it also makes the foam more pliable.)

2 Using the knife, cut off the bottom ends of three of the candles to varying lengths. Push the candles into the centre of the foam. Alternatively, you could use one single, large candle.

3 Cut the eucalyptus into pieces about 15 cm (6 in) long. Insert the stalks in the foam to cover it.

4 Cut the hellebore flower stems to about 13 cm (5 in) long and add to the arrangement at random intervals.

CABBAGE decoration

Ornamental cabbages have wonderfully coloured leaves that deserve to be used in indoor decorations. This design is simple to achieve, using a base of florist's foam soaked to keep the leaves fresh. The cabbage leaves are arranged in two layers, face up and face down.

YOU WILL NEED
- large, sharp knife
- block of florist's foam
- candle
- plate
- ornamental cabbage

1 Cut a square block from the florist's foam large enough to hold the candle, leaving a margin of about 1 cm (½ in) all around. Soak the foam in water, drain, then place it in the middle of the plate. Push the candle into the centre.

2 Trim away the top of the block all around the candle. Break the leaves off the cabbage and, working from the bottom, push them face up into the outer side of the foam.

3 Repeat with a top layer, placing the underside of the leaves uppermost to make them fan away from the candle.

SCENTED
arrangement

A heady mix of scented herbs and leaves makes a traditional decoration around the base of a classic candlestick. Allow the leaves to bend and twist naturally, at the same time building up the rounded shape of the candle ring. You could also include other cottage garden plants.

YOU WILL NEED
- 15 cm (6 in) diameter florist's foam ring
- candlestick
- scissors
- small quantities of rosemary, lemon geranium leaves, fennel, hyssop and violas

1 Soak the florist's foam ring in cold water and place it over the candlestick. Start the arrangement by making a basic outline in the foam with stems of rosemary and lemon geranium leaves, positioning them evenly around the ring. Place the leaves at different angles to produce a fuller effect.

2 Fill the gaps evenly with fennel and hyssop, and finally add a few fresh violas or other cottage flowers for colour.

CHOOSING HERBS
Select herbs that are as fresh as possible. Choose ones that will blend in with any particular flowers you like.

candle basket

For a special dinner party, create a luscious display of fruit and roses, making your own selection of materials according to the season. Choose fruits or berries to complement the colour of the roses – rose hips with red or orange roses, and green berries with white or cream roses.

YOU WILL NEED

- piece of florist's foam, cut to fit snugly in the bowl
- plastic bowl
- string (optional)
- wire basket
- green moss
- wooden skewer
- 8 roses
- selection of small branches with small fruits
- 6 poppy seedheads
- 3 small rolled beeswax candles

1 Soak the florist's foam in water until completely saturated. Wedge it into the bowl, securing it with string, if necessary. Place the bowl in the wire basket and cover it thoroughly with green moss.

2 Make holes at random in the foam with a wooden skewer. This prevents foam particles becoming lodged in the flower stems, which will stop them taking up water. Begin the arrangement, pushing in the foliage and poppy seedheads.

3 Place the roses randomly, trying to place them in the holes in the foam that were made with the skewer. Keep turning the basket around as you work to see the effect from all sides. Then add the candles, pushing them in securely, and making sure that no foliage or flowers will be near the flames once lit, to avoid a fire hazard.

FESTIVE
candle pot

Simple materials make a very attractive pot for a Christmas decoration in this fresh-looking display. The white roses and glossy red berries are set off beautifully against the dark green ivy leaves, collected in the woods. A few stalks of trailing variegated ivy lighten the effect.

YOU WILL NEED

- small terracotta flowerpot
- chicken wire
- large, sharp knife
- florist's foam ball, to fit the pot
- candle
- green ivy
- white roses
- red berries
- variegated trailing ivy

BELOW Fruits, such as pomegranates and apples, are also wonderful at Christmastime.

1 Place the pot in the centre of a square of chicken wire. Bring the wire up around the pot and bend it into place.

2 Cut the florist's foam ball in half and soak one half.

3 Place the foam in the pot, cut-side up so you have a flat surface. Place the candle in the centre of the pot.

4 Arrange green ivy leaves all around the candle, to provide a lush, dark green base for the other decoration.

5 Add a few white roses as a focal point, and bunches of red berries.

6 Add more roses and intersperse variegated trailing ivy among the green ivy leaves.

L E A F Y
garland

Tiny crab apples and oak leaves make a lovely, country-style table decoration, with the glorious colour of the apples accentuated by tall, tapered candles, secured in a ring of florist's foam. Allow the arrangement to dry out naturally and make a lasting display.

YOU WILL NEED

- 25 cm (10 in) diameter florist's foam ring
- 4 tapered candles
- secateurs (pruners)
- crab apple branches
- pin oak leaves

1 Soak the foam ring in water. Set the candles into the foam. With secateurs (pruners), cut small bunches of crab apples off the main stems.

2 Push in the stems of the oak leaves around the ring into the foam. Add smaller sprays on the inside.

3 Finally, attach the crab apple bunches, placing them directly on top in a decorative arrangement.

candelabra

For a special occasion, make novel use of a candelabra by bringing it down to table level. Rich white lilies and purple asters make a stunning combination, and the trailing ivy adds a more informal touch. Tall rolled beeswax or white church (ivory pillar) candles add a grand touch.

YOU WILL NEED

- 30 cm (12 in) diameter florist's foam ring
- candelabra
- scissors
- 20 short stems viburnum
- 20 short stems variegated pieris
- 15 heads Easter lily
- 10 stems purple aster
- 3 pieces variegated trailing ivy
- tall rolled beeswax candles

1 Soak the florist's foam ring in cold water and position the candelabra within the ring. Cut approximately 10 cm (4 in) long stems of viburnum and variegated pieris. Push them into the foam to create an even foliage outline.

2 Trim the lily heads, leaving about 7.5 cm (3 in) of stem to push into the foam. Group the heads in threes around the circumference of the foam ring.

3 Separate the main stems of the asters from any side stems with flowerheads. Cut all the aster stems to approximately 10 cm (4 in) and distribute them evenly through the arrangement, pushing them firmly into the plastic foam.

4 Push the cut ends of the variegated ivy into the soaked florist's foam, then entwine it around the candelabra. For safety reasons, do not allow any ivy leaves to come up over the candleholder's wax guards.

HERB
candle ring

The frothy white flowerheads and yellow-green leaves of scented dill are used here on their own to make a lovely fresh summer garland, studded with nightlights (tea-lights). The centre of the display is filled with terracotta pots containing other herbs such as rosemary and mint.

YOU WILL NEED

- 30 cm (12 in) diameter florist's foam ring
- 2 blocks florist's foam
- 4 terracotta pots
- cellophane
- scissors or craft knife
- white dill
- herb plants (eg rosemary, mint, marjoram)
- red berries (eg cranberries or rosehips)

1 Soak the florist's foam ring thoroughly in water and leave to drain. Press the nightlights (tea-lights) into the foam, making sure that they are equally spaced around the ring.

2 Soak the blocks of florist's foam and drain well. Line the terracotta pots with cellophane to prevent leakage. With scissors or a craft knife, cut the florist's foam blocks to fit tightly and snugly into the pots.

3 Mass the dill around the ring between the nightlights (tea-lights). Fill the pots with herbs and foliage. Position the base ring and arrange the pots inside it. Add a sprig of coloured berries.

HERB POTS
After the party, the candle ring can be dismantled and the individual pots of herbs may be used separately indoors.

SIMPLE table display

For a simple, colourful display, group potted plants together, then link them with coloured nightlights (tea-lights) placed on leaves. As well as being an attractive decoration, the large leaves will catch any dripping wax. Choose flowering plants in different heights and colours.

YOU WILL NEED

- small decorative plants (eg viola, ornamental cabbage, African violet, cyclamen)
- selection of terracotta flowerpots, in different shapes and sizes
- bun moss
- nightlights (tea-lights), in various colours
- large leaves

1 Remove the plants from their containers and re-pot in terracotta pots. Water well, then cover the compost in the pots with moist moss. Set aside to drain thoroughly.

2 Arrange the pots on the table. Place the nightlights (tea-lights), singly and in clusters, on large leaves around the group of pots.

C I N N A M O N
advent candle

Make the most of a slow-burning church (ivory pillar) candle by marking off the days of December until Christmas Day. Light the Advent candle each day to burn down to the each of the 25 cinnamon sticks and remove each one as the days progress to avoid the display catching fire.

YOU WILL NEED

- 25 medium cinnamon sticks
- 7.5 x 23 cm (3 x 9 in) church (ivory pillar) candle
- raffia
- scissors
- 10 cm (4 in) diameter florist's foam ring
- stub (floral) wires
- reindeer moss
- 20 dried red rose heads
- florist's adhesive

1 Attach the cinnamon sticks to the outside of the candle, tying them on with the raffia.

2 Position the cinnamon sticks in reducing height, so that they spiral around the candle from the tallest at the top to the shortest at the bottom, which should be approximately 6 cm (2½ in) long. The excess lengths of cinnamon will overhang the bottom of the candle. Bind the cinnamon securely with raffia at two points, tying it in a bow. Cut off the excess lengths of the cinnamon sticks, so that the sticks are all flush with the base of the candle.

3 Push the cinnamon-wrapped candle into the centre of the foam ring. Make hairpin shapes from the stub (floral) wires and use to pin the moss on to the foam to cover the ring completely.

4 Cut the stems of the roses to 2.5 cm (1 in). Add a little adhesive to the bases and stems of the roses. Push them into the florist's foam through the reindeer moss, to create a ring around the candle.

centrepiece

Traditionally, four Advent candles are burned for an hour on each Sunday leading up to Christmas. On the first Sunday, one candle is burned for an hour. On the second Sunday it is burned alongside the second candle, and so on. This idea inspired this lovely centrepiece.

YOU WILL NEED

- block of florist's foam
- plate
- 4 church (ivory pillar) candles
- bunch of tree ivy
- picture-framer's gilt wax
- scissors
- wire-cutters
- fine wire
- 10 Chinese lanterns

1 Soak the florist's foam brick in water and set it on a plate. Carefully push the candles into the foam.

2 Gild the ivy berries with picture-framer's gilt wax. Cut the tree ivy stems to size and push them into the foam.

3 Cut some lengths of fine wire. Pass a wire through the base of each Chinese lantern and twist the ends together. Push the twisted wire ends into the foam base around the candles, to make an even and attractive arrangement.

VARIATION
You could also use rolled beeswax candles instead of church (ivory pillar) candles for this attractive table centrepiece, as they burn slowly too and also give off a subtle and delicious aroma of honey.

F E S T I V E
decoration

A group of five or six church (ivory pillar) candles look very handsome displayed on a mantelpiece, especially when the candlelight is reflected in a mirror. Here the creamy white candles are perfectly complemented by the cream and green tones of variegated ivy and pale green moss.

YOU WILL NEED

- polystyrene balls
- double-sided adhesive (cellophane) tape
- scissors
- reindeer moss
- church (ivory pillar) candles of various heights and widths
- foil dishes (pans)
- plastic adhesive
- stems of variegated ivy
- florist's wire

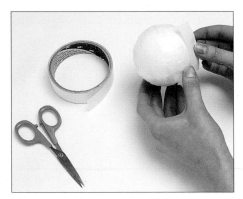

1 To make the moss balls, cover the polystyrene shapes all over with double-sided adhesive (cellophane) tape.

2 Press the moss gently on to the balls, covering them completely.

3 Arrange the candles by standing them in an attractive arrangement on foil dishes (pans). Secure the candles firmly with pieces of plastic adhesive attached to their bases.

4 Wire together small bunches of ivy and attach them to a longer main stem. Arrange the candles on the mantelpiece and drape the ivy in front. Position the moss balls around the candles.

WEDDING display

For a really romantic traditional wedding, place these lovely decorations on the ends of the pews down the church aisle. The posies have a summery look, but are made of dried flowers so can be created at any time of year. Keep the flower stems fairly long to balance the tall candle.

YOU WILL NEED

- 2 garden canes, each about 60 cm (24 in) long
- tall church (ivory pillar) candle
- strong plastic tape
- scissors
- dried pink larkspur
- dried pink roses
- stub (floral) wires
- raffia bow
- strong wire

1 Place a cane on either side of the base of the candle. Hold them firmly in place with tape, as tightly as possible.

2 Arrange a layer of flowers around the candle, with the heads just above the height of the tape, holding them in place. Continue adding flowers.

3 Criss-cross the stems at an outward angle to produce a wide, circular display. Tie a stub (floral) wire around the stems and fasten firmly. Tie a raffia bow around the middle to cover the wire. Attach a strong S-shaped wire at the back to attach the display to the pew.

templates

In order to enlarge the templates to the size that you require, trace the template and draw a grid of equal-sized squares over your tracing. Measure the space where the shape is to go, then draw a grid to these proportions, with an equal number of squares as appear on your tracing. Take each square individually and draw the relevant parts of the pattern in the larger square. Alternatively, you can enlarge your tracing on a photocopier.

Cut-out Paper Lanterns
(triangular lantern)
(reproduced at 80%)

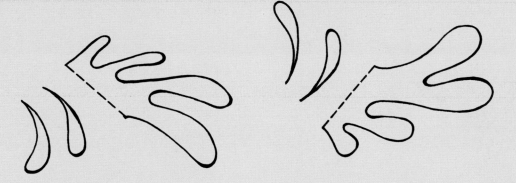

Rope Candleholder
(reproduced at 73%)

Cut-out Paper Lanterns
(cylindrical lantern)
(reproduced at 80%)

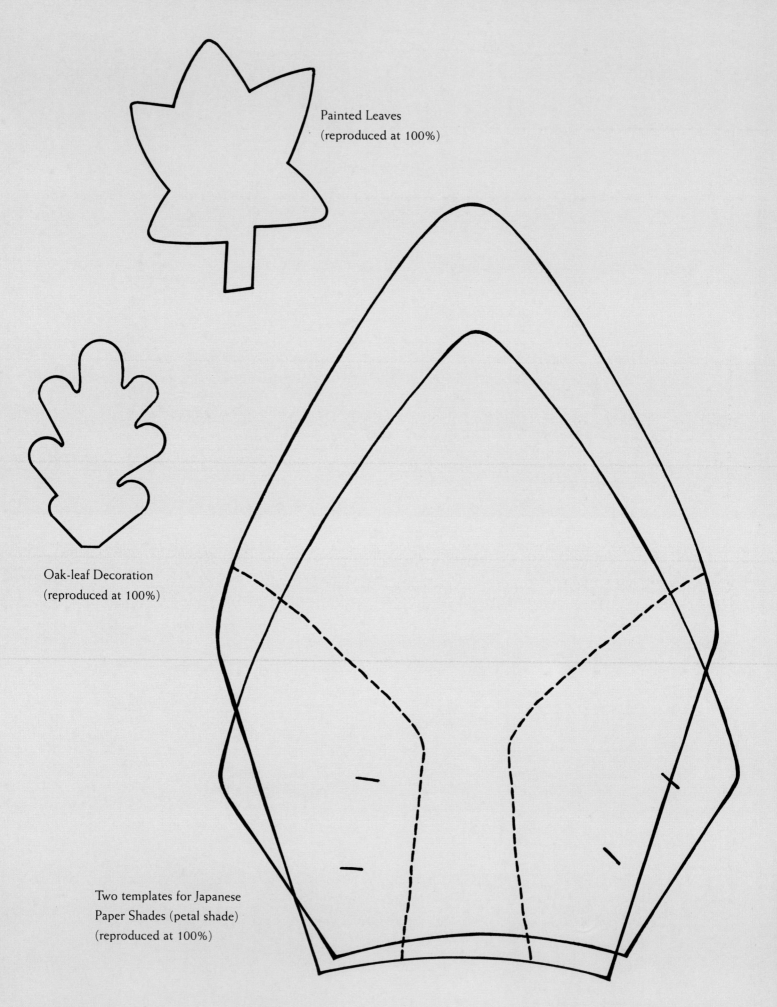

Painted Leaves
(reproduced at 100%)

Oak-leaf Decoration
(reproduced at 100%)

Two templates for Japanese
Paper Shades (petal shade)
(reproduced at 100%)

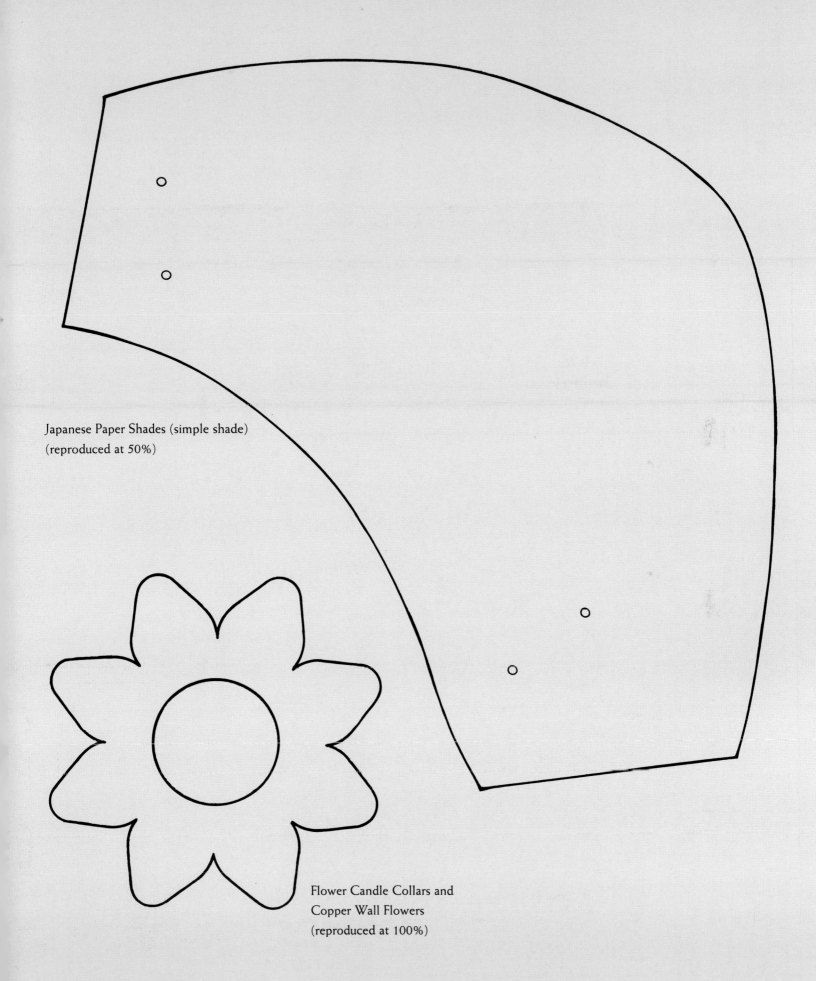

Japanese Paper Shades (simple shade)
(reproduced at 50%)

Flower Candle Collars and
Copper Wall Flowers
(reproduced at 100%)

Folk-art Pumpkin Lantern
(adjust according to size of pumpkin)

Coiled Wire Sconce
(reproduced at 73%)

Wall Sconce
(enlarge to required size)

suppliers

A wide range of candles and candle accessories is available from very many shops and stockists. This selection of addresses is a compilation of some particularly useful suppliers that were, in particular, of great assistance in this publication.

UNITED KINGDOM

Angelic
6 Neal Street
London WC2H NLY
(0171) 240 2114
Wide range of candles and accessories available.

Candle Maker's Suppliers
28 Blythe Road
London W14 0HA
(0171) 602 4031
Everything you will need to make your own candles. Mail-order service with catalogue also available on request.

Point a la Ligne
Michael Johnson (Ceramics) Ltd
81 Kingsgate Road
London NW6 4JY
(0171) 624 2493
Exquisite shaped candles, accessories and modern ceramic candlesticks available.

UNITED STATES OF AMERICA

Barker Enterprises, Inc.
15106 10th Avenue
SW Seattle
WA 98166
(206) 244 1870
Candle-making supplies: dyes, waxes, glaze. Candle moulds in over 650 shapes.

Candlechem Co.
PO Box 705
Randolph
MA 02368
(617) 986 7541
Candle-making chemicals, scents, dyes, pigments, perfume, essential oils and others.

Candleshtick
2444 Broadway
New York
NY 10024
(212) 787 5444
A wide selection of classic as well as novelty candles. Paraffin, beeswax and moulds, scents and dyes also available.

Dick Blick
PO Box 1267
Galesburg
IL 61402
(309) 343 6181
General craft supplier. Catalogue available on request.

Pottery Barn
Mail Order Department
PO Box 7044
San Francisco
CA 94120-7044
(800) 922 5507
Mail-order catalogue features a wide range of various shapes and sizes of candles, candlesticks, and stencil kits, patinas and crackle glaze. There are also various stores in major cities nationwide that can be visited.

Pourette Manufacturing, Inc.
681 Roosevelt Way NE
Seattle
WA 98155
(206) 525 4488
800-800-WICK (9245)
Range of candle-making supplies is available.

CANADA

Charlotte Hobbys
782 Shield Road
Hemmingford
Quebec J0L 1H0
(516) 247 2590
Kits and candle supplies.

AUSTRALIA

The Craft Company
272 Victoria Avenue
Chatswood NSW 2067
(02) 413 1781
Waxes, wicks, dyes and moulds.

Hornsby Beekeeping Supplies
63a Hunter Street
Hornsby NSW 2077
(02) 477 5569
Bulk and coloured wax, and wicks.

Janet's Art Supplies
145 Victoria Avenue
Chatswood NSW 2067
(02) 417 8572
Candle-making kits and beeswax.

John L Guilfoyle Pty Ltd.
772 Boundary Road
Darra QLD 4076
(07) 375 3677
Also at 23 Charles Street
St Marys NSW 2760
(02) 623 5585
Also at 299 Prospect Road
Blair Athol SA 5084
(08) 344 8307
Pure beeswax, coloured beeswax, bulk beeswax and candle wicks.

Mr Craft
Coolung Lane
Eastwood NSW 2122
(02) 858 2868
Paraffin wax, wicks, colours, moulds and books.

NEW ZEALAND

Askew
(09) 358 1825
Bedingfields
(09) 367 6881
Bloomsbury Galleries
(09) 357 0889
Corso De Fiori
(09) 307 9166
Country Road Homewear
(03) 366 7870
French Country Collections
(09) 634 7230
Gondwana International
(03) 477 6909
Indigo
(09) 302 0737
Levene
(09) 274 4211
Makum Textiles
(09) 379 3041
Marr Antiques and Interiors
(09) 309 7787
Masterworks Gallery
(09) 309 5843
Sanderson
(09) 309 0645
The Design Merchants
(09) 303 3188

acknowledgements

The publisher thanks the following
for their contributions:

CONTRIBUTORS

Deborah Alexander, (p150);
Michael Ball (pp41b, 140-1), Fiona
Barnett and Roger Egerickx
(pp34b, 185, 234, 239-42), Deena
Beverley (p35bl), Penny Boylan
(pp31tl, 144-5, 148bl, 16l, 174-5,
181, 244, 252), Diana Civil (pp5tr,
45tr, 49r, 63t, 74br, 76-7, 80t, 91,
93,98-9, 100bl, 106-9, 110bl, 112-
3, 120bl, 124-5, 146-7, 156-7, 164-
5, 168-9, 194-7, 212-3, 255), David
Constable of The Candle
Workshop, Gelligroes Mill,
Gelligroes, Pontallanfraith,
Blackwood, Gwent, (pp14-5, 110-1,
116-8), Stephanie Donaldson (pp2,
3, 12, 18t, 29t, 44, 46b, 61l, 62l,
63b, 64b, 44b, 62, 65tl+tr, 78l, 96-
7), Marion Elliot (pp18b, 19, 1119,
54-5, 216-7), Tessa Evelegh (pp9t,
10-11, 13tr, 22tl, 23, 25t, 26b,
28br, 34tl, 45tl+b, 47b, 49l, 56b,
59b, 60t+b, 61br, 67tr+r, 68-9, 70tl,
71, 80l, 81tr+b, 82r, 83b, 84tl, 90,
96br, 130, 136-7, 182-3, 192-3,
198-9, 202-6, 200-1, 218-9, 228-9,
231-3, 236-7, 238, 243), Lucinda
Ganderton (p158-9, 176), Emma
Hardy (pp122, 138-9, 180, 224-5),
Stephanie Harvey (pp17r, 28l),
Jessica Houdret (38t), Gilly Love
(pp70b, 79, 81, 84b, 123, 128b, 235,
253), Mary Maguire (pp21tl, 75t,
126-7, 140bl, 148-9, 152-3, 160-1,
170-1, 178-9, 210-11, 214-5),
Terence Moore (p27br, 37br,
38t+b, 40b, 41t, 184, 186-91, 230,
245), Deirdre O'Malley (pp27bl,
64t, 208-9), Sandra Rangecroft,
Forever Flowering, Orchard
House, Mortlake Road, Surrey
TW9 4AS (p57t), Deborah
Schneebeli-Morrell (pp24b, 120-1,
162-3, 166-7, 172-3, 222-3),
Andrea Spencer (pp13tl, 70l, 142-
3), Liz Wagstaff (pp9br, 35tr+br,
126bl, 17tl), Stewart and Sally
Walton (65b) and Pamela Westland
(pp22br,.35br, 36t+b, 58br).

PHOTOGRAPHERS

Michelle Garrett (pp2, 3, 12, 27br,

29t, 35bl, 37br, 38b, 40b, 41t, 44,
56b, 60b, 61l, 70b, 79, 80l, 81, 84b,
96-7, 123, 128b, 182-4, 188-91,
218, 230, 235-7, 245, 253), Janine
Hosegood (pp16l, 174-5, 181, 244),
Lizzie Orme (pp27bl, 64t, 208-9),
David Parmiter and Lucy Tizzard
(pp154-5, 216-7), Spike Powell
(pp70l, 13tl, 142-3), Graham Rae
and Rodney Forte (pp144-5, 252),
Russel Sadur (pp5tr, 45tr, 49r,
74br, 80t, 76-7, 63t, 91, 93,98-9,
100bl, 106-9, 110bl, 112-3, 120bl,
124-5, 146-7, 156-7, 164-5, 168-9,
194-7, 212-3, 255), Steve Tanner
(p65b), Peter Williams (pp17r, 18b,
19, 21tl, 28l, 41b, 140-1, 152-3,
210-11) and Polly Wreford (pp22tl,
23, 26b, 28br, 34tl, 45, 47b, 49l,
59b, 60t, 61br, 68-9, 70tl, 71, 81tr,
83b, 84tl, 90, 96b, 130, 136-7, 231).

STYLISTS

Katie Gibbs and Georgina Rhodes.

ADDITIONAL CREDITS

Many thanks to the following for
supplying materials for this book:
Arco, 25 Calvin Street, London E1
6NW; Price's Patent Candle
Company Ltd, 110 York Road,
London SW11 3RU; Bougies La
Francaise, UK subsidiary, LDX
Marketing Ltd, 19e Grove End
Road, London NW8 9SD; Kirker
Greer & Co., Belvedere Road,
Burnham-on-Crouch, Essex CM0
8AJ; Candlewick Green, Units 1 &
2 Donnington Park, Birdham Road,
Donnington, Chichester, West
Sussex PO20 7DU; The Candle
Shop, 30 The Market, London
WC2E 8RE; Pebeo, Philip & Tacey,
Northway, Andover, Hampshire
SP10 5BA; Plastikote Ltd, London
Road Industrial Estate, Sawston,
Cambridge CB2 4TR; The Dining
Room Shop, 62-64 White Hart
Lane, London SW13 0PZ;
Verandah, 15b Blenheim Crescent,

London W11 2EE; Sebastiano
Barbagallo, 15-17 Pembridge
Road, London W11 3HG; Past
Times, Witney, Oxford OX8 6BH;
Graham & Green, 4 & 7 Elgin
Crescent, London W11 2JA; Neal
Street East, 5-7 Neal Street,
London WC2H 9PU; Nice Irma's,
46 Goodge Street, London W1P
1FJ; Shaker, 25 Harcourt Street,
London W1H 1DT; Paperchase,
213 Tottenham Court Road,
London W1P 9AF; Purves &
Purves, 80-81 & 83 Tottenham
Court Road, London W1P 9HD;
Janet Fitch, 25a Old Compton
Street, London W1V 5PL; Mildred
Pearce, 33 Earlham Street,
London WC2H 9LD; Avant Garden,
77 Ledbury Road, London W11
2AG; Aero, 96 Westbourne Grove,
London W2 5RT; Gore Booker, 41
Bedford Street, London WC2E
9HA; Diane Flint, 84a Moray Road,
London N4 3LA; Junction
Eighteen, Bath Road, Warminster,
Wiltshire BA12 8PE; Hilary Lowe,
(available from) George Clark, The
High Street, Stockbridge,
Hampshire; Global Village, 17 St
James Street, South Petherton,
Somerst TA13 5BS; Golfar &
Hughes, Studio C1, The Old
Imperial Laundry, 71 Warriner
Gardens, London SW11 4XW;
Poole Pottery Ltd, Poole, Dorset
BH15 1RF; Royal Creamware,
Junction 31, M62 Motorway WF6
1TN; Mary Rose Young, Oak
House, Arthur's Folly, Parkend, Nr
Lydney, Gloucester GL15 4JQ;
William Sheppee Ltd, 1a Church
Avenue, London SW14 8NW;
Yilmaz Uslu, Flat 8, 21 Seymour
Street, London W1.
Thomas & Wilson, for plaster
mouldings; Aynsley China Ltd, for
fine bone china; Yorkshire Fittings
Ltd, for plumber's fittings; Tobias
and The Angel for hyacinth
glasses; and Alison Jenkins for
the Rope Candlesticks, Wire
Candle Sconce, Japanese Paper
Shades and Paper Lanterns.
t=top, b=bottom, r=right, l=left.

index

Figures in italics refer to
captions for photographs.